___TRANSFORMATIONAL___
___RADICAL RESU___

CHARLES E. SMITH PH.D.

"Life is either a daring adventure or nothing at all. Security does not exist in nature, nor do the children of men as a whole experience it. Avoiding danger is no safer in the long run than exposure."

Helen Keller

"For a revolution to be successful, it has to follow the three-act structure of a play. The first act establishes the characters and the plot, the second act sharpens the conflict, and in the third act, 'good and evil have their dramatic confrontation and resolution.'"

Saul Alinsky, American activist

THIS BOOK IS FOR ANYONE COMMITTED TO WHAT THEY WANT BUT NOT CONFIDENT THEY CAN GET IT..., AND WHO ARE WILLING TO GO ALL THE WAY.

**Copyright© 2022. Charles E Smith Ph.D.
All Rights Reserved.**

No part of this work covered by the copyright herein may be reproduced or used in any form or by any means—graphic, electronic or mechanical without the prior written permission of the publisher. Any request for photocopying, recording, taping, or information storage and retrieval systems of any part of this book shall be directed in writing to the author.

Acknowledgment

I love who I love in my family and the wise people I've been privileged to meet and find genius in the connection.

Kathy Smith, Marcia Smith, Marilyn Smith, Meaghan Smith, George Michael Smith, Jonathan Lewis Smith, Lillian Smith, Rose Smith, Tony Turnbull, Ron Bynum, Lew Epstein, and Don Duprey are always with me, and many others in a Buddhist flow of life-giving moments.

Contents

Acknowledgment ii
Testimonials vii
PREFACE - WHERE DID WE GO WRONG? xi
IT'S ALL ENERGY, AND IT'S ALL YOU xiv
TRANSFORMATION IS NOT CHANGE 1
REAL THINKING COMES FROM RECOGNIZING FREQUENCY 5
WE ALL LIVE ON A RESERVATION 8
THE BEST COUNTRY MONEY CAN BUY? 9
TRANSFORMATION CALLS FOR A NEW WAY TO SEE THE WORLD 11
ENERGY LANGUAGE 11
MUTUALITY LANGUAGE 11
CURIOSITY LANGUAGE 12
THE MIND OF ALBERT EINSTEIN 17
UNIFIED FIELD THEORY—THE HUMAN HEART . 20
EINSTEIN QUOTES 22
TRANSFORMATION IS LIKE STEPPING OFF A CLIFF 24
TRANSFORMATION IS A LANGUAGE FOR ADVANCED FREEDOM 26
MUTUALITY AND THE OVERVIEW EFFECT 29
THE EXPERIENCE OF THE OVERVIEW EFFECT 32

MASTERY OF FLOW 35
MASTERY OF ENERGY IN FOCUS 38
1. DEEP-ROOTED PASSION 39
2. CLEAR, MASSIVELY TRANSFORMATIVE PURPOSES (MTPs) 39
3. SINGULAR, UNWAVERING FOCUS 39
4. FIRST PRINCIPLES THINKING 39
5. THINKING IN PROBABILITIES 40
6. NOT SETTLING—NOT GIVING UP 41
RADICAL TRANSFORMATION CALLS FOR MACH 25: ESCAPE VELOCITY 42
The Mach 25 Movement: Achieving Escape Velocity 43
FAILURE IN ACHIEVING ESCAPE VELOCITY: POSSIBILITY DEFICIT DISORDER 45
FEAR IS THE MIND KILLER 50
COMMITMENT TO RADICAL TRANSFORMATION: THE GENIUS OF FERNANDO FLORES 51
1. Commitment 52
2. What's Missing? 52
3. What's Missing that Gets What's Missing to be Missing? 53
4. Committed Speaking 56
OBLIQUE SHAFTS OF ILLUMINATION 58
POSSIBILITIES 62
DAGAZ 64
THE POWER OF US 66

THE TALKING STICK	68
DIALOGUE	71
CONNECT AND MOVE ON	72
THERE IS NO SECRET INGREDIENT…ONLY YOU	73
CHARACTER IS DECISIVE	75
UNCHARACTERISTIC RESULTS REQUIRE UNCHARACTERISTIC ACTION	77
PERFORMANCE AND SOCIETAL BREAKTHROUGHS THAT EXPLODE CULTURAL LIMITS ON WHAT'S POSSIBLE	79
JOSEPH CAMPBELL AND THE TRANSFORMATIONAL POWER OF MYTHOLOGY	81
GRATITUDE VIDEO	82
HUNA SCIENCE	83
THE MERLIN FACTOR: THINKING FROM THE FUTURE	85
THE MERLIN FACTOR: AVALON AND GLASTONBURY	87
THE "CALLING:" ENERGY THAT EMBRACES	88
HARMONY THROUGH CONFLICT	93
SUSTAINABILITY	95
COACHABILITY	96
COACHING	97
THE VALUE OF BEING USELESS	98

CARL SAGAN'S BALONEY DETECTION KIT 100

COMMON FALLACIES OF LOGIC AND RHETORIC 101

CONSIDER: THE WORLD IS WHAT YOU THINK IT IS 103

THE COLLABORATIVE ENERGY QUOTIENT (CEQ): A Self-Directed Assessment Of Your Behavior And Capacity For Collaboration With Others 104

PRACTICAL APPLICATIONS 107

Article 1: The Camp David Retreat, ... 107

Article 2: Mastering What Transforms: Dream the Impossible Dream and Go for It 108

Article 3: Breaking Free: Bringing the Overview Effect to Life and Work 110

Article 4: Conversations that Matter 111

Testimonials

"Charles Smith has distilled a lifetime of truth-seeking into a fascinating book that spans ancient to modern wisdom. There is something in this book for everyone: philosophers, educators, students, executives, artists, scientists, and more. Charlie's own writings are woven into the various sections of the book and provide a practical enhancement to the quotes from the great transformational leaders of the past and present.

Charlie has been my mentor, my friend, my colleague, and my inspiration for the past thirty years. While serving as a Department of Defense Program Executive, I asked Charlie to help with the National Aerospace Plane Program. He constantly used the Mach 25 goal to define what we were capable of achieving and was a force for innovation.

After leaving the government, I joined him in his consulting company and partnered with him to create profound change in government and business organizations. Later, we created the Collaborative Innovation Institute to develop transformational collaborations aimed at solving some of the most challenging problems in the world. His persistent vision and voice of the Overview Effect as a stimulus for inspiring international collaboration has led to some real breakthroughs in science, business, and government. Charles Smith is a national treasure and a man of great imagination and tremendous intellect."

Robert Barthelemy
Founder, The Wright Brothers Institute
and The Collaborative Innovation Institute

"I started working with Charlie Smith when I came to Canada as the General Manager for the Novartis Consumer Health business in 2010. It was an unbelievable opportunity with a great company and great talent. I was most interested in how to transform the 'good' into the 'great.' I asked around to meet people that had helped to create real transformation in the workplace and met Charlie.

He and I shared the belief that true integration (mentally, emotionally, organizationally, socially, culturally, and ecologically) is the most challenging and most powerfully effective strategy for endless expansion..., and we could offer no greater value proposition or service to a company.

In the next two years, we moved the whole company on a path beyond the ordinary. We drove a high performance-based team toward a truly human culture, delivered three times market growth, and over-delivered against internal targets significantly. Working with Charlie was one of the most enriching experiences of my professional life."

> Dominique Giulini, Vice President,
> Global Head Ethics and Compliance,
> GSK Consumer Health

"I thought you guys would appreciate some great feedback. You may recall our target of £100m, and you may even remember how some of the Team thought I was on drugs and this was mission impossible! Well, the good news is, I am pleased to say we hit it a year earlier than expected, which is fantastic news, and I would like to thank you for your positive contribution and involvement in achieving this. Technically, we disbanded the old KC last summer, but Sean reconstructed the account, hence the reason why I'm able to give you the good news."

Kind Regards, Kevin Walsh,
Chief Executive

"The first time I met Charlie Smith, I was struck by the profundity of his insight, indeed wisdom. His emphasis on the central importance of human energy in accomplishment echoes my own research and experience on high-performance individuals, companies, and nations. Energy is the result of will, will is an expression of aspiration, aspiration is the artesian well that awakens inspiration and creativity in human beings. The highest achievement in every field is the result of focusing the energy through high goals and values to transform it into force and channeling that force through effective organization and highly motivated and skilled individuals. It's an eternal formula for sustained success.

Garry Jacobs, CEO
World Academy of Art and Science

"Radically novel insights! Dr. Smith's book is certain to stretch your mind and effectiveness as a leader—and as a person."

Daniel L. Shapiro, Ph. D, Director,
Harvard International Negotiation Program and
author, Negotiating the Nonnegotiable

"Charlie Smith has a profound ability to dig into the depths of the human condition and unearth practical solutions that not only transform the individual but are also essential for creating a thriving planet."

Andrew Hewitt, Founder,
GameChangers 500

"The world is what you think it is, and Charlie's insights may profoundly transform how you see it and yourself."

Kent Jones,
Marketing and Results Consultant

"Charlie Smith is the quintessential 'deep thinker' ...a philosopher for our time. Provoking deep thought in others is his superpower! What is so wonderful and compelling about this book is his writing style, and storytelling makes his insights accessible and relatable. You will take this journey with Charlie and recognize yourself as a "deep thinker" as well!"

Jackie Eiting, Master Counselor,
and Organizational Development Expert

"Charles Smith has always sought to create a possibility where it doesn't exist as he helps people take deep dives into what's true and expand the boundaries of our reality. This book takes you on that voyage."

Nadine B Hack, CEO,
BeCause Global Consulting

PREFACE - WHERE DID WE GO WRONG?

What is normal and what's acceptable in training, in school, in family, religion, hierarchy, in what's appropriate on the street, with friends and strangers in social company, and what is necessary for promotion and recognition in business and public activity, generally includes what is:

- familiar
- sensible
- logical
- linear
- not confusing
- evidence-based
- faith-based
- measurable
- not paradoxical
- reasonable
- not oblique
- grounded in familiar frequencies

What's considered inappropriate is:

- unpredictable
- unreasonable
- surprising
- desirable but impossible
- escape velocity
- sharing feelings that might rock the boat

What's left is usually:

- Conventional behavior
- Conventional logic
- Conventional listening
- Conventional speaking

What is limited is imagination, uncharacteristic behavior, and possibility; the very necessities for Transformation ("a thorough or dramatic change in form or appearance").

Energy is Decisive

Forever, I've looked for one idea that brings dramatic change. Along the way, I met a talented philosopher and teacher named Victor Sanchez, who studied ancient Toltec Indians in South America, and their culture based on the insight that *"People with the most available energy will prevail."* Anybody, anyplace going to pieces, has less and less energy. Einstein said that *"underneath everything is energy, bouncing balls of vitality. Energy is all there is."* This is a novel perspective on a well-established idea—the huge importance of human energy for success.

Everywhere, from where I grew up in Boston to where I had worked across America and England, in the prevailing cultures of Judaism, Christianity, Business, Mathematics, Competition, Getting the Job Done, Making Money, going One Step at a Time, Winning, Obeying the Rules, Being a Good Boy or Good Girl–that's what life was about.

I write this book as a summary of what my life has been deep down:

- To help people get along better.
- To create a possibility where it doesn't exist.
- To help people take deep dives into what's true.

IT'S ALL ENERGY, AND IT'S ALL YOU

"That's The Whole Key, Your Relationship with Yourself… that's the Stairway to The Stars, To Heaven. You Are the One…get That Part Right, and Everything Is Yours, Everywhere, Always, and no matter who you seem to be with or the perception you may be experiencing…Your Self Is Senior To any and all of that polar, yo-yo, oppositional distortion…that is the optical or mental delusion Einstein refers to, which is not the defining essence… Reality Is, Your Reality, The Reality We Share, and Through Conscious Active Cooperation, we Can Remember This Again and by Doing So Recover The Essential Life and Living that we have been unwittingly depriving ourselves of…This Is the Conversation of Utmost Importance and Priority for Us All if we are To Really and Truly Innovate Collaboratively and Rise Up Out of the dark and confusing hole we've been unnecessarily loitering around in…We Powerfully Need and Require everyone's Help Here… I Need You, Bro… Way More than you can possibly imagine…and our Meeting is no coincidence or matter of amusing curiosity…You and I Have Enormous Opportunity in our Friendship, More than You or I can or even consider in separate thinking…."

Jeffery Mironov, Recording Artist,
Philosopher & Teacher

TRANSFORMATION IS NOT CHANGE

To "Change" is to substitute or replace something, like changing a flat tire. Transformation is "a thorough or dramatic shift in form or appearance." Some examples include:

- A caterpillar turning into a butterfly
- The first man landing on the moon
- Women getting the right to vote
- Developing a cure for Polio
- The Wright Brothers creating and flying the first airplane
- Meeting your first Love

Mastery of Transformation requires the ability to see, hear and act on certain frequencies. A Frequency is not an idea; it's more like a way of listening and looking at things. It's more like being open to something that's not there but could be there. It's like a language you never studied. You might recognize it as German, French, Italian, or Spanish but don't have a clue as to what it means.

The effect of Transformation is a sudden, dramatic insight. It's a way of seeing something or suddenly seeing something that you haven't already seen. For example, I never heard the word "Commitment" until I was 43 years old. It never came up in my family, or schooling, or with friends. It wasn't like people were against it; it just wasn't a "Frequency" they could hear, a language from which they could make sense, a language from which they could think.

Governments, institutions, businesses, families, and communities, quietly and when they deem necessary, avoid

Transformation like the plague. Transformation tends to scare authorities and threatens their power to control what they are certain needs to be controlled.

People are promoted to high positions for many reasons, including to assure that the values, practices, and requirements of the existing system stay in place and remain intact. The result is that "Curiosity" tends to be limited or disappears entirely. The flow, grace, honesty, human contact, and creativity that has the system grow in the first place diminishes, along with the energy needed for creativity and growth.

This phenomenon remains unspeakable, and energy is spent protecting the power, position, and beliefs of the people in charge. So, the only way these people and these places can persist and grow is through the quiet use of force, rules, expectations, money, and fear, most of which is not directly in people's faces. But it doesn't produce the energy and vitality needed, wanted, or desired to keep making the company and the world a better place.

I've tried to explain this to people, and most of the time, their eyes cross. It's like asking them to parachute into unknown territory where yesterday, today, and tomorrow are all happening at once, where what it took to do well or get by was not a necessity, and suddenly seeing what was fixed and certainly was actually malleable.

Transformation is not logical in the way most of us were trained to know what logic is, what common sense is, pleasing the people around you or the people you love, or other people you want to influence. For me, there have been thrilling, improbable Transformational exceptions like the ending of World War Two when I was a child, getting into Harvard

College while I was about to flunk out of high school, America landing on the moon, cures for malaria and polio, and what happened with miraculous effect when I started listening to people who were smarter, more educated, more honest, and braver than me.

The search for Transformation reminds me of the quest for the "Holy Grail." A lot of people have been looking for it for a long time and never quite found it. Many people like the idea of Transformation but are stuck with what they already know. Especially where they've already succeeded, they are afraid to imagine and execute what doesn't already exist.

I was recently at a conference of brilliant academics talking about the necessity for Transformation in the United States and around the world. Proposals were offered. Examples were concrete and imaginative but, in my view, not Transformational.

People talk a lot about the need for transformation but often don't mean it or stop meaning it as soon as the original driving breakdown is resolved. When resolution happens, most won't continue to bring anything they're afraid of into play. Most will revert to their previous ways of operating. They forget where the magic came from and avoid the continuing necessity for Curiosity and Mutuality. People stop paying attention to levels of their own and others' energy. They forget or dismiss the importance of uncertainty, and the power of flow, instead of always being intentional.

Patience, silence, minimum explanation, unqualified positive regard for participants, and the importance of providing uncharacteristic insight go unseen. How come? Does the absence of uncharacteristic behavior enable people in power to stay in power?

Early in my career in organizational behavior, I was hired by one of the largest and most successful consumer goods companies in the world. The first meeting was confusing; people didn't agree on what was important, and there was little progress. Someone asked, *"What's really going on here?"* An older and wiser member said, *"The only way to explain what goes on here is that the real purpose is to keep the people in power in power..., to keep what actually happens in the hands of those with real power in the first place."*

The insight stays with me. The United States government was supposed to be run by farmers and community leaders who would come to Washington D.C. or their state capitals for a while and then go back to their homes and jobs. Now, the idea is to stay in Washington forever. This is explained by saying that the longer you stay, the better you get, the more experienced and insightful you can be for The People, and it's good to have consistent people be there for a long time.

We seem to spend much of our time trying to solve the wrong problems. What's the right question here? Is this a fool's errand? I'm not a revolutionary. A lot of people in power deserve to be in power; they are competent, honest, smart, creative, thoughtful, and concerned for people. What is the right question?

REAL THINKING COMES FROM RECOGNIZING FREQUENCY

A Frequency lets you hear or see something. For example, understanding English is the frequency that lets you understand English. A frequency is not an idea, not a goal, not a subject-object sentence, not a cognitive event. Kathy always looks for a positive reality. Jon always looks for a scientific or logical solution. I always look for a way out.

Technically, a frequency is the number of occurrences of a repeating event per unit of time. It's also the rate at which a vibration occurs that constitutes a wave or a flow.

Examples of frequency-driven realities:

- If we are living together in a small village with little contact from the outside world, we may never find out what is real outside.
- My son thinks that much of the current virus conversation is a scam and refuses to get vaccinated. I think that countless people are going to the hospital, and I'm afraid for my son's life.
- I said to my wife's cousin's 5-year-old, a beautiful little girl named Sophie, that in ancient Greece, thousands of years ago, there was a goddess named Sophia. In an instant, she said with force, "NO.., Jesus created everything." The conversation was over, and who was I to argue.
- I was born to Jewish parents and grandparents. We lived in Dorchester, Massachusetts. where everyone I knew was Jewish. I never met non-Jews. Sometimes, I'd hear stories about Irish people from other parts of Boston coming to beat us up. This was scary and

never happened. The Frequency remained real in my mind.

Is any of this Real, or is the world what I think it is?

- My grandfather was a Russian immigrant and kept telling me that women were dangerous and that I needed to be careful and in charge all the time. Was this real? Just because he said it was real for him, it became real for me.
- My wife's father lived in a small town in Ohio and told me that small towns were better than big cities. He believed it. I never did.
- Fundamental True Believers, Christians, Jews, Muslims, Atheists, Capitalists, Communists, etc., are certain about who is God and who isn't.
- My CEO friend once said, *"Profit was everything."* Sitting on his giant Arabian horse farm sipping fine wine, it both seemed strange, and how could I argue?
- In a wonderful Peter Sellers movie, someone asked, *"Does your dog bite?"* Sellers said no, and then the dog bit the man who'd asked. Sellers then said, *"That's not my dog."*
- Then, there's my dear friend Patrick, a practicing Roman Catholic and a kind man who only judged people by whether they were thoughtful and kind or not. Pat lived in a "Paradox"—two realities in which he truly believed in the Divinity of Jesus and truly believed that how people treat each other is what's most important.

Is there such a thing as "Real Thinking," or are billions of people thinking that what they're thinking is real, with massive, misguided effects on marriages, families, companies, foreign relations, hatred, cruelty, happy times, and misunderstanding?

WE ALL LIVE ON A RESERVATION

I have a Native American friend who lives in the Taos Pueblo in New Mexico. He is a famous, talented musician, songwriter, flutist, and philosopher. At lunch a few months ago, he mentioned something about the reservation. I said something in response, and as always happens when I say something about Indian life, he said a decisive, "NO." And then, "Everyone everywhere lives on a reservation."

As I've thought about this, the truth of it came home. White men, white women, black men, black women, rich people, poor people, religious people, political people, businessmen, people always in small towns, people always in cities, businesswomen, true believers everywhere..., we all live on reservations..., pieces of mental land with boundaries, hard and fast beliefs, and conversations you can't have with anyone who doesn't live on the reservation. And it's impossible to ever really leave the reservation, at least mentally and often physically.

Real thinking is that almost everyone lives on a reservation. Almost every one of us is sure that our reality is real. Our "reservation" is the boundary of our reality.

THE BEST COUNTRY MONEY CAN BUY?

Is your country sustained by a housing and rental system based on what people can afford? Is it sustained by hotels that raise the rent during busy seasons just because they can? Is it sustained by parents who support their children's education based on the money they expect to make? Is it equivalent to a national religion where God is money, and the rest do as well as they can manage? For most, rich or poor, money is the "reservation," the arbiter of personal freedom, healthcare, life expectancy, access to justice, quality of housing, media, self-worth, and so on.

I've spent much of my life making good money and never paying attention to the game being played. Now at age 86, I don't have the energy to ignore the game and am finding other ways to keep our family's ship afloat. But experience moves from unpleasant to rotten for too many people. I've listened to and not argued against the arguments for why this is a good idea. "Work hard, be creative, make friends, get a great education, don't complain, play the game, don't break the rules, help keep the people in power stay in power—stay inside the political, educational, economic, social, and familial Electric Fences." I've lived in this culture for my whole life, enjoyed the money, and never realized or criticized the game being played.

Where it's missing, there must be a better possibility, a better reality. This would be a reality in which people and life itself would be more important, or at least as important as money, for anybody with an obvious moral character.

I've wondered for years why nobody writes poems or love songs about corporations. I've wondered why so many people and executives I've coached and befriended in corporations don't like their jobs and think of happier and more creative ways to spend their time. I believe that Democracy is a very positive idea that only goes partway. We need to invent a way that serves life before money.

TRANSFORMATION CALLS FOR A NEW WAY TO SEE THE WORLD

This formula, "E=MC^2," inspired by Einstein's work, has produced remarkable results and positive culture change in countless individuals, companies, teams, agencies, governments, and initiatives in ways that are demonstrable across many of the world cultures, but not codified in much of the western world's language.

ENERGY LANGUAGE comes from the strength and vitality required for sustained physical or mental activity and connection with others. Synonyms include vitality, vigor, life, liveliness, animation, vivacity, spiritedness, verve, enthusiasm, zest, vibrancy, spark, sparkle, effervescence, ebullience, exuberance, buoyancy, sprightliness.

MUTUALITY LANGUAGE—the density of the Space between people varies from completely clear/transparent/open/empty to completely dense/closed/blocked/full. Mutuality is a continuous area that is relatively free, available, or unoccupied with the quality or state of being mutual. Attitudes, values, principles, beliefs, thoughts, fears, emotions, ideas, preconceptions, orientations, cultures, and identities can occupy the space.

Mutuality reduces the density of the space between people and makes the Space between people less dense by introducing: Breathing (alone or together), Present Awareness, Overview Consciousness, the Ability to shift the mindset from victim to cause in the matter, and Intense presence of nature, questions that create new possibilities,

Embracing Paradox, Promising what you cannot predict, Meditation, Absence of Force, Absence of Explanation, Absence of Transaction, Generous Listening, Speaking from the Heart, Committed Speaking, Eliminating Noise, Contemplation, the Intent to "Inter-Be," Beginner's Mind, Zero Gravity, Not being a Noodle in Someone Else's Soup.

CURIOSITY LANGUAGE is the urge to know more about something. The state of being curious includes an inquisitive interest in others' concerns, wondering, and being ready to poke around and figure something out. In mathematics, a square is a result of multiplying a number by itself, e.g., two times two. In Curiosity among individuals or groups, squaring is the acceleration of the experience of mutual wonder such that "I" becomes "Us."

Accelerating Curiosity is an energetic phenomenon. Its nature is neither linear nor conceptual. What does curiosity consist of?

- Curiosity for information
- Curiosity for play
- Curiosity for possibility and meaning

Curiosity can be applied to any situation with three simple steps:

- Be interested: "That's interesting."
- Ask: "What is this really about?"
- Wonder: "What can I create with this?"

Richard Hill, www.richardhill.com.au

In Creativity and Collaboration, the main thing is Curiosity, finding common ground, listening generously, asking questions, and having new freedom to choose.

The biggest barrier is my self-importance, which I think I already know. The only refuge I have for self-importance is to know that there is no refuge. There is no escape except to transform myself into the refuge of "us," the power of being together.

I talk every week to my friend Tony Turnbull. We connect and move on to the next thing. I cannot tell where I stop, and he begins. His identity and my identity do not get in the way.

Years ago, it never felt safe enough, relaxed enough. I had to be the cause of things. The magic seems to come from being awake to what is happening at this exact moment. Just being there. No agenda.

There had been bits and glimmers over the years. A program at the Gestalt Institute of Cleveland opened new ideas and practices. These make sense of my life work in a thrilling new way. This was not from a plan but from a way I could not explain.

Being Curious is interest in figuring something out. Curiosity is squaring the acceleration of wonder, internal vibrational energy in the mind and body. The absence of Curiosity in the core of individuals and groups inhibits the possibilities of shared leadership and recombining processes in symbiotic or flowing relationships.

Conflict and misunderstanding are almost everywhere, from feeling uneasy to withholding what's true for you, to disagreement, to avoidance, to suffering, to hatred, to getting even, to isolating, to punishing, to killing off what you don't like, one way or another. In paying attention to the Future of Innovative Collaboration, what matters the most is how people are being with and treating each other. This book is about the possibility of creating systems, cultures, and relationships where peoples' experience is more important, or at least as important as money or authoritarianism..., and where companies make money.

As a young man growing up in my family, there was no Collaboration and no Innovation. Every day it was the same stories, rules, religious activities, and warnings that the world was full of poisoned berries. I became cautious and didn't know it. High school and college ended up as versions of people and places where I didn't have fun and not where I belonged. The purpose of too many days was to get through them.

I had the privilege of going to a fine college and business school and never liked most of it. I kept going back to more schools in the hope of learning something that would make me happy and found myself in another college going for an advanced degree…and I didn't like that either.

Then, I stumbled into a postgraduate evening program at the Gestalt Institute of Cleveland, with teachers and students that made me feel at home and with language that said they cared about what I really cared about, even though I didn't yet have the words for it. I didn't have to believe anything and felt in my blood that what they were saying and doing was true and real for me and the life I already had.

For the first time in my life, I was having experiences and meeting people that made sense of who I was already and taught me a new language that created possibilities and examples for the kind of life I really wanted but could not even imagine having. Without knowing it, for the first time in school and most anywhere, I had the experience of "Unconditional Positive Regard" for what I deeply cared about and never knew.

Psychologist Carl Rogers invented the idea that everyone has vast resources for self-understanding, altering how they see themselves, their attitudes, and self-directed behavior…and you can only tap into those resources from the experience of unconditional positive regard. Rogers believed that "Unconditional Positive Regard" from others was necessary for healing and growth.

This experience changed my life, created a career, and opened me up to unknown futures well beyond the weekly Lone Ranger radio programs that gave my earlier inspiration. It was my first experience of Collaboration, a new antenna that helped me listen to what was a better world. For me, after that, there was only one thing: I saw that Innovative Collaboration means finding common ground, common identity, listening generously to each other, asking questions, and even for a few moments finding new freedom to choose.

The only refuge I've found from my own self-importance is to know that there is no refuge, no escape, except to transform myself into the refuge of "us," the power and the release of being together and creating together. What happens is that I usually discover that my emotional and mental obstacles aren't real.

"A woman or a man goes to knowledge as they go to war, wide-awake, with fear, with respect, and with absolute assurance. Going to knowledge or going to war in any other manner is a mistake, and whoever makes it might never live to regret it."

Carlos Castaneda,
The Teachings of Don Juan

THE MIND OF ALBERT EINSTEIN

Albert Einstein said, *"Everything is energy, and that is all there is to it. Match the frequency of the reality you want, and you cannot help but get that reality. It can be no other way. This is not philosophy; it is physics.*

Concerning matter, we have all been wrong. What we have called matter is energy, whose vibration has been so lowered as to be perceptible to the senses. Matter is spirit reduced to the point of visibility. There is no matter."

Consider that Albert Einstein's philosophy is a Transformational Frequency and an Energy Field from which we can create the meaningful difference we need where it seems impossible.

An energy field in physics is a force field, a vector field, that describes a non-contact force acting on a particle at various positions in space. In the modern framework of the quantum theory of fields, an energy field occupies space, contains energy, and its presence precludes a classical "true vacuum."

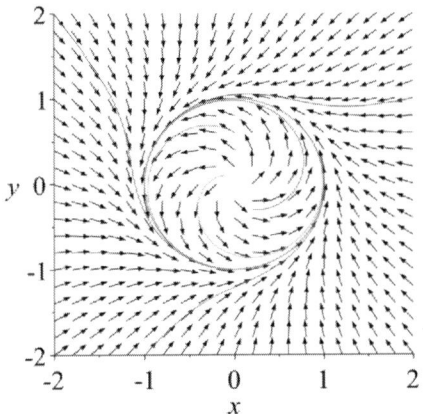

https://commons.wikimedia.org/wiki/File:Vector_field_and_trajectories_of_a_simple_limit_cycle.svg

This has led physicists to consider electromagnetic fields to be a physical entity, making the field concept a supporting paradigm of the edifice of modern physics.

"The fact that the electromagnetic field can possess momentum and energy makes it very real ... a particle makes a field, and a field acts on another particle..., and the field has such familiar properties as energy, content, and momentum, just as particles can have."

(Richard Feynman, https://www.feynmanlectures.caltech.edu/I_10.html)

One idea central to what I've learned about Transformation is that *"Systems with the Most Human Energy Will Prevail."* This is the Presence of Aliveness and consists of:

- Shared Power
- Spirit
- Dynamism

- Connection
- Touching
- Generous Listening
- Breathing
- Moving
- Looking
- Compassion
- Breathing
- Inner light

This can be a new bottom line for business, education, government, healthcare, and social justice. The goal to consider is that once and for all, the possibility is always possible. This is your life, and your choices do not belong to anyone else. Now is the moment of power, the world is what you think it is, and Freedom is to keep doing what you are afraid of.

UNIFIED FIELD THEORY—THE HUMAN HEART

Some scientists are now postulating that "The Unified Field" theory Einstein was grappling with when he died may recognize that the energy field emanating from the Planck units in the human heart creates a much larger field (up to 8 feet around the body) than those in the brain–a possibility that human consciousness is sourced as much from the heart as the brain and that it overlaps/interacts with other energy fields.

Energy Awareness comes from attending to, sensing, and directly working with the patterns of energy present in relationships, teams, organizations, businesses, and communities. It reveals underlying patterns that directly affect the success of any effort and helps a leader to:

- Sense the blocks to creating high-energy teams, projects, or organizations.
- Understand natural solutions or innovations that "want to emerge" and are consistent with the players' passions.
- Unlock the energy and wisdom that is naturally present.
- Discover ways to heal, create partnerships, and navigate complex situations.
- Build loyalty and agreement to shared goals.

In business and in life itself, Energetic Awareness happens in a specific context—a mission-driven or relationship-driven framework. It has the power to mobilize everyone involved. Energy Awareness occurs in a moment of presence. It propels people, groups, and ultimately systems forward by literally seeing themselves and the related environment at its very core as a field of interacting opportunities and energy flows.

EINSTEIN QUOTES

"I didn't arrive at my understanding of the fundamental laws of the universe through my rational mind."

"Time does not exist–we invented it. Time is what the clock says. The distinction between the past, present, and future is only a stubbornly persistent illusion."

"I think 99 times and find nothing. I stop thinking, swim in silence, and the truth comes to me."

"The intellect has little to do on the road to discovery. There comes a leap in consciousness; call it intuition or what you will; the solution comes to you, and you don't know how or why."

"When you examine the lives of the most influential people who have ever walked among us, you discover one thread that winds through them all. They have been aligned first with their spiritual nature and only then with their physical selves."

"One thing I have learned in a long life: that all our science, measured against reality, is primitive and childlike. We still do not know one-thousandth of one percent of what nature has revealed to us. It is entirely possible that behind the perception of our senses, worlds are hidden of which we are unaware."

"Everything is determined, every beginning and ending, by forces over which we have no control. It is determined for the insect, as well as for the star. Human beings, vegetables, or

cosmic dust, we all dance to a mysterious tune, intoned in the distance by an invisible piper."

"I am happy because I want nothing from anyone. I do not care about money. Decorations, titles, or distinctions mean nothing to me. I do not crave praise. I claim credit for nothing. A happy man is too satisfied with the present to dwell too much on the future."

TRANSFORMATION IS LIKE STEPPING OFF A CLIFF

Radical Education means a mindset change for teachers, students, and parents. Most people like what they're used to. Years ago, my sons were in a new school in Orlando, Florida, designed for Radical Education based on insight and participation from several universities. Many of the parents hated it as it was so different from their own experience. The same was true for many teachers, and officials were under pressure to keep everybody happy. It wasn't long until the school reverted to the ABCs with little attention to the imagination.

Radical Education evokes imagination and possibility thinking rather than information and content. Radical education does not eliminate content but stops it from dominating imagination. This can feel like chaos in the classroom, going beyond teacher limits, and the need to legitimize both Flow and Intention.

I had an experience of Radical Education in my freshman year at Harvard College in a course about the nature of science. The teacher began by presenting "Cosmology"—what the world was thought to be like 5000 years ago. He presented it in the present tense, and it was the truth. For example, stars were all stuck to an invisible globe in the sky. Students rebelled and told him he was wrong, and the earth was really moving around the sun. The teacher ignored these comments and made a case for a perfect reality of how it looked 5000 years ago. That was the whole class.

Rather than revisit what happened the week before, in the next class, he presented how the universe really operated

4000 years ago. When students reminded him of last week's class, he ignored them and insisted on all of the elements of reality 4000 years ago, and was utterly convincing. This went on for weeks, with him advancing to a different time in history and presenting that reality as it was then, arguing with students who disagreed. The teacher always won the argument.

In the very last class of the semester, the teacher asked, "What is Science?" What came out was that *"Science is a set of concepts and conceptual schemes arrived at through observation and experimentation," which led to another set of concepts and conceptual schemes."* This went on forever as a never-ending inquiry into what's really going on based on the current capacity to observe, analyze and imagine.

I felt free with a gratifying sense of freedom and believed that we will never really know what's ultimately going on and can only pursue that reality to the best of our ability. That was Radical Education based on the extraordinary consciousness of the teacher, from which he was able to penetrate the very way that students saw reality.

TRANSFORMATION IS A LANGUAGE FOR ADVANCED FREEDOM

Extraordinary transformational teacher Werner Erhard said, *"You have to want transformation as much as you want your own next breath."*

The human spirit seeks to be free, and a system or organization needs to be ordered and controlled. On the one side is the legitimate fear of unbridled violence as in the novel "Lord of the Flies," which can follow from too much freedom. On the other hand, is the legitimate fear of domination, injustice, and cruelty from arbitrary authority.

I suggest that Advanced Freedom means that whenever there is a choice, each individual needs to create one of the alternatives for themselves…, and each individual needs to learn to listen independently to their automatic mind and their imagination.

Do we need a new and Transformational way of seeing things and language that lets large numbers of people have a radical experience, a radical insight that creates a new possibility for them and the future they want for who and what they love? It's a way of looking, seeing, and listening…, away from which Transformation is simply a natural way for them to live and assures a world of societal transformation and peace with justice. I'm suggesting a way in which Transformation, a societal relationship-based language, is available for business and life.

"The task is gigantic if we are to prevent more personal and international tragedies based on unpredictability, insecurity,

fears, and anxieties which are steadily disorganizing the functioning of the human nervous system. Only when we face these fears and build from the ruins intelligently may we save for future civilizations whatever there is to save..., a new and intelligent move forward."

Alfred Korzybski. <u>Science and Sanity</u>, Institute of General Semantics, Fifth Edition, 1995.

Alan Watts says in <u>The Book on the Taboo Against Knowing Who You Are</u>: *"Thus the 'brainy' economy designed to produce this happiness is a fantastic vicious circle which must either manufacture more and more pleasures or collapses— providing constant titillation of the ears, eyes, and nerve ends with incessant streams of almost inescapable noise and visual distractions. The perfect "subject" for the aims of this economy is the person who continuously itches his ears with the radio, preferably using the portable kind which can go with him at all hours and in all places. His eyes flit without rest from television screen to newspaper, to magazine, keeping him in a sort of orgasm-with-out-release through a series of teasing glimpses of shiny automobiles, shiny female bodies, and other sensuous surfaces, interspersed with such restorers of sensitivity—shock treatments—as "human interest" shots of criminals, mangled bodies, wrecked airplanes, prize fights, and burning buildings.*

The literature or discourse that goes along with this is similarly manufactured to tease without satisfaction, to replace every partial gratification with a new desire. This stream of stimulants is designed to produce cravings for more and more of the same, though louder and faster, and these cravings drive us to do work that is of no interest save for the money it pays—to buy more lavish radios, sleeker automobiles, glossier magazines, and better television sets, all of which will somehow conspire to persuade us that happiness lies just around the corner if we buy one more."

MUTUALITY AND THE OVERVIEW EFFECT

Frank Herbert said that *"..., in all the universe there is only the insatiable appetite of matter..., that energy is the only true solid, and energy learns."*

Such learning is always the sum of intellectual, physical, emotional, and spiritual activity. We can get very smart cognitively yet remain stupid emotionally, spiritually, or physically. In an energetic paradigm, responsibility begins with our willingness to be cause-in-the-matter of energy across the entire system.

Edgar Mitchell, Sixth Man on The Moon, said, *"There was a startling recognition that the nature of the universe was not as I had been taught. I not only saw the connectedness, I felt it. I was overwhelmed with the sensation of physically and mentally extending out into the cosmos. I realized that this was a biological response of my brain attempting to reorganize and give meaning to information about the wonderful and awesome processes that I was privileged to view."*

The Overview Effect is the Awareness that the whole of anything is greater than the sum of its parts. The Overview Effect is a cognitive shift in awareness reported by many astronauts and cosmonauts during space flight. It refers to the experience of seeing first-hand the reality that the Earth in space is a tiny, fragile ball of life 'hanging in the void,' shielded and nourished by a paper-thin atmosphere.

This consciousness is often accompanied by a sense of wonder, awe, and curiosity. On breaking free of Earth's gravity and going to space, some astronauts experienced a surprising change in their perspective of life on Earth. Many discovered a compelling drive within themselves to help make business, government, healthcare, and the world as we know it a better place.

> Frank White: The Overview Effect:
> Space Exploration and Human Evolution
> (1987/1998/2014/2021)

The Overview Effect often transforms astronauts' perspective on the planet and humanity's place in the universe. Some common aspects of it are a feeling of awe for the planet, a profound understanding of the interconnection of all life, and a renewed sense of responsibility for taking care of the environment.

Dr. George Robinson was my colleague, and a privilege to meet and write an article together. He served as Legal Counsel at the Smithsonian Institution in Washington, D.C., where he enjoyed an exceptionally broad law practice relating to the Smithsonian's worldwide pursuit of scientific research. He also served as an International Relations Specialist for the National Aeronautics and Space Administration (NASA).

He told me that artists are those that interpret the unknown long before the sensibilities of the common, the mainstream, perceive its touch. Artists live the future before that future appears. It's getting close now. The artists know it. Space migration, resettlement on distant worlds, an earthly planet unable to support humanity. In theoretical physics—wormholes, black holes, quantum theory, and relativity is still unreconciled.

He said that the movie, *Interstellar* admirably dealt with all these challenges. Hand in hand with the science consultants, both artists and scientists did a magnificent job of explaining not only physics but also philosophy. He said that while both teams meshed the complexity into manageable understanding for a lay public, the storytellers must be commended for weaving the movie together, using the dimension of Love to describe a deeper dimension beyond our 4-dimensional reality of time and space.

Interstellar told the story of humanity's salvation wrapped not only around the concrete realities of 4-dimensional space/time physics but around also the story of intelligence that offered insight into a higher dimensional reality, where space and time were but artifacts of materiality given to explore as an access pathway to a greater possibility, an understanding of something more, something larger, something infinitely more real.

> *"Consider that center of the universe is everywhere. It is surrounded by a light blue aureole that gradually darkens, becoming turquoise, dark blue, violet, and finally coal black."*
>
> Yuri Gagarin, Cosmonaut,
> First Human in Space

THE EXPERIENCE OF THE OVERVIEW EFFECT

Astronaut Story Musgrave told me that while many just went and did their jobs, most of the astronauts who experienced the Overview Effect were people already open to possibility, transcendence, poetry, and relatedness.

The Overview Effect seems like when I relax into my experience of the Grand Canyon, the stars at night, my children's faces, how my wife is being, and the Black Forest Mountains in the mist. Awe, ineffability, wonder, mystery, and uplifted spirit come from being present to the experience of the whole being greater than the sum of the parts. Being is everywhere.

Edgar Mitchell said about those who did experience the Overview Effect, *"You develop an instant global consciousness, a people orientation, an intense dissatisfaction with the state of the world, and a compulsion to do something about it. From out there on the moon, international politics look so petty. You want to grab a politician by the scruff of the neck and drag him a quarter of a million miles out and say, 'Look at that, you son of a bitch.'"*

What is the Overview Effect? It is a deep, personal, profound experience that radically alters one's worldview and the nature of reality. It is the awareness that the whole of a situation is greater than, or other than, the sum of its parts. This consciousness is often accompanied by a sense of wonder, awe, and curiosity.

It can allow you to break free from the grip of your personal gravity and move forward where you have been stuck, thwarted, putting up with, and not believing in your dream of the future. The Overview Effect is a gateway to completely changing the way something is thought about or done. It is a gateway between linear thinking, where step-by-step progress is required, and Quantum Mind, where everything is possible now.

> *"I don't know what I'm supposed to do. I only know what I can do."*
>
> Star Trek

Watch the videos on Google or an appropriate link.

- Frank White's Harvard Overview Effect Symposium (one hour plus)
(http://www.youtube.com/watch?v=0X_fhLIPydE)

- The Vimeo Overview Video (25 minutes)
(https://vimeo.com/55073825)

MASTERY OF FLOW

Vincent Van Gogh, Starry Night

My wife and I recently went to a Vincent van Gogh exhibit in Los Angeles. I was immediately struck by how he created his work, his art. It was almost entirely Flow, movement, color, and animation. There was intention in the image. You could tell there was a village and a sky. But the overall experience was Wonder, Awe, and a kind of mystery.

The moment of Transformation is like a moment of Zero Gravity and Flow. A person who generates energy adds to the Flow. Consider that where you don't start with and end with "Flow," it causes depletion, divisiveness, or conflict. In the modern world, intention, analysis, and measurement are King, and "Flow" too often comes later, if at all.

Transformation requires Awareness of the rate at which vibration occurs in yourself and others. Transformation is a Frequency; it doesn't come from an idea, a subject-object sentence, or a cognitive event. Like German, you have to know German to make sense of it.

INTENTION AND FLOW. George Michael Smith, Glass Artist, *and* Charles E Smith

Nature Flows, Relationships Flow, Creativity Flows, Spirituality Flows, Love Flows. Intention, analysis, and measurement are often useful, but as the diverse nature of human realities becomes increasingly unarguable, intention without flow seems to stifle the possibility of being free for all human beings.

A person flying an airplane in the sky versus driving a car on the road—what's the difference? When driving on the road, there are certain inherent factors that affect the path one travels. Weather, daylight, and all sorts of road conditions become variable that may delay or arrest the journey. Roads only work if you stay on them, either because it's the guide to the destination or because there are likely barriers or ditches keeping the car on the road. The road is your course. If a tree falls across the road, it is likely you will have to backtrack and either wait or take a detour. This type of travel has an intention to arrive at its destination but is unable to flow with the physical space it is in.

If the travel is by flight, then there are inherently different factors that affect one's path. When flying, the destination may still be a fixed point, but flying allows for a universe of Flow, which can be marked by a series of waypoints that exist in free space. The intention is held in the mind (of both pilot and computer), while the flow exists in the way the aircraft gets from point to point. The path between each waypoint is the course. One may drift a few feet away from the course before correcting or many miles. If there is a storm or danger, waypoints can be changed to create a different course that can still lead to the same destination. Rather than backtracking, a flight plan allows for the detours needed to be part of the forward movement. One means staying on a fluid course with small adjustments vs. being bound by the conditions of a "single, permanent course."

MASTERY OF ENERGY IN FOCUS

A couple of years ago, I was driving a friend through Houston, TX, on the way to MD Anderson, a cancer hospital. It was our first visit, and the traffic was dreadful. I was on edge and not used to such heavy city congestion. All of a sudden, there was a huge sign on the side of the highway, perhaps 20 yards high and another 20 yards wide, that said, *"MD Anderson: We Only Do Cancer."* It was the simplest, most powerful sign I'd ever seen.

It was "singularity," bringing unity out of diversity. There was no definition, only clarity, power, and direction. Here was a declaration in the face of possibly dire circumstances that MD Anderson was dedicated to and aimed at the singularity of energy in every aspect of what they did and what they stood for. The medical visit was successful.

Elon Musk is a master of bringing energy into focus. It is all energy, and it's all him. His six principles bring extraordinary focus to the opportunity of extraordinary results. There is no visible wobble.

Musk is currently CEO of SpaceX and Tesla. He has various goals toward which he works through his ventures. These include redefining the automobile industry with electric cars, making renewable energy compete with traditional sources, making space travel affordable, and enabling the colonization of Mars and the development of safe artificial intelligence to benefit humanity.

For his various contributions, Musk has received numerous honors, including the Gold Space Medal from the World Aeronautical Federation (FAI); and being elected a Fellow of the Royal Society (FRS). Many of his accomplishments seem impossible, such as firing a rocket into space and having it reliably return and land safely in the same place.

Musk's Principles for achieving such results are explained by his friend, Peter Diamandis. They are straightforward, sensible, and practical:

1. DEEP-ROOTED PASSION—Only tackle those problems where you have deep-rooted passion and conviction.

2. CLEAR, MASSIVELY TRANSFORMATIVE PURPOSES (MTPs)

3. SINGULAR, UNWAVERING FOCUS— Passion, purpose, and focus. All of these put you into what psychologists call a flow state: a highly enjoyable and meaningful state where work ceases to become work and instead becomes energizing and immersive. This intensity is different from the kind of intensity that burns people out or causes them to quit jobs. This intensity is energizing—not draining.

4. FIRST PRINCIPLES THINKING—First principles thinking is a mode of inquiry borrowed from physics that is designed to relentlessly pursue the foundations of any given problem from fundamental truths.

Musk says, *"I think it is important to reason from first principles rather than by analogy. The normal way we conduct our lives is we reason by analogy. [When reasoning by analogy] we are doing this because it's like something else that was done, or it is like what other people are doing—slight iterations on a theme.*

First principles is a kind of physics way of looking at the world. You boil things down to the most fundamental truths and ask, "What are we sure is true?" and then reason up from here.

Somebody could say, "Battery packs are really expensive, and that's just the way they will always be. Historically, it has cost $600 per kilowatt-hour. It's not going to be much better than that in the future.

With First principles, you say, "What are the material constituents of the batteries? What is the stock market value of the material constituents? First-principles thinking works so because it gives us a proven strategy for editing out complexity and allows us to sidestep the tide of popular opinion."

5. THINKING IN PROBABILITIES—*"Outcomes are usually not deterministic...they're probabilistic. But we don't think that way. The popular definition of insanity—doing the same thing over and over and expecting a different result—it's only true in a highly deterministic situation which most situations are. "Thinking in probabilities" has a 60 percent chance of success—rather than deterministically—if I do A and B, then C will definitely happen—doesn't just guard against oversimplification. It also protects us against the brain's inherent laziness.*

However, outcomes exist across a range. "The future is not certain. It's really a set of branching probability streams." How Elon chooses which streams to explore depends on the relationship between those probabilities and the importance of his objective.

"Even if the probability for success is fairly low if the objective is really important, it's still worth doing. Conversely, if the objective is less important, then the probability needs to be much greater. How I decide which projects to take on depends on probability multiplied by the importance of the objective."

SpaceX and Tesla are great examples. When Musk started both companies, he thought their probability of success was less than 50 percent—probably a fair bit less than 50 percent. Elon Musk points out, *"I also thought these were things that needed to get done. So even if the money was lost, it was still worth trying."*

6. NOT SETTLING—NOT GIVING UP

RADICAL TRANSFORMATION CALLS FOR MACH 25: ESCAPE VELOCITY

The James Webb Space Telescope launched into space aboard an Ariane 5 rocket on Christmas morning from the French Guiana Space Center,
Jody Amiet/Agence France-Presse—Getty Images

Mach 25 is escape velocity. It is the speed and energy it takes to break free from the grip of gravity on Earth and go to low space orbit or outer space. In the National Aerospace Plane project, the US Air Force, NASA, and several aerospace companies and agencies created a project led by Dr. Robert Barthelemy to design an airplane that would take off from a runway and reach Mach 25—Escape Velocity and be able to land again.

Over several years they made great strides in a new world of innovation and progress. Then the program was canceled by Congress. A primary lesson was that people could create miracles, moonshots, unbelievable progress, and collaboration when the committed goal is beyond any existing possibility.

The Mach 25 Movement: Achieving Escape Velocity

The Mach 25 Movement applies lessons from the scientific breakthrough of achieving escape velocity together with transformational thinking to enable individuals to achieve what they really want in work and life but are not confident they can get.

The Mach 25 Movement is a global group of individuals applying lessons learned by men and women in going into space and applying them to Collaborative Innovation and Breakthrough Thinking, where you really care about work and life on earth. The capacity to generate Escape Velocity is necessary for Real Thinking.

- Escape Velocity becomes available from observing people's relationships and work in terms of Vibrational Resonance.
- As personal Energy Expands, Escape Velocity improves vis-a-vis the world around you.
- Escape Velocity comes from attending to, sensing, and directly working with the patterns of energy
- present in relationships, teams, organizations, businesses, and communities.
- Escape Velocity comes from sensing the blocks to creating high-energy teams, projects, or organizations and understanding natural solutions or innovations that "want to emerge" and are consistent with the players' passions.
- Escape Velocity happens in a moment of presence. It propels people, groups, and ultimately systems forward by literally seeing themselves and the related

- environment at its very core as a field of interacting opportunities and flows.
- We can get very smart mentally yet remain thoughtless emotionally, spiritually, or physically. Escape Velocity is Breaking Free of current circumstances. (In the next moment, another set of gravitational forces may need to be contended with—i.e., gravity).

Mastering Escape Velocity brings you to Zero Gravity, Advanced Freedom, and the ability to Freely Choose. The problem is that Zero Gravity doesn't last. There are always new forces to deal with, such as the gravity of the Sun after you've reached the Moon...and each of us has hardwired habits and beliefs from our own past that don't go away.

My friend Lew Epstein said, *"It's all about Recovery."* There are a number of ways to recover Escape Velocity, and they require a never-ending commitment to Recovery. The place where we have a victim-based mindset is the gravity that keeps Escape Velocity and Radical Education in check.

FAILURE IN ACHIEVING ESCAPE VELOCITY: POSSIBILITY DEFICIT DISORDER

Charles E. Smith
Publisher Joseph F. Paris Jr., a recognized thought leader in Operational Excellence.
November 11, 2009, in XONITEK

Possibility Deficit Disorder (PDD) is the pervasive and persistent experience of 'no possibility' now and no exceptional prospects in the future. This can account for both the absence of Radical Education and the opportunity to introduce Mach 25.

PDD is widespread in modern times. At a national level, it is evidenced in the lack of ambitious ventures in industrial policy, necessary education resources, infrastructure planning, national security, and transportation. PDD can be observed at the corporate level in ineffective product development, low employee morale, low customer loyalty, high staff turnover, lack of cooperation between functions, self-protective behavior between individuals, and distrust between hierarchy and employees. PDD is demonstrated in individual lives in lack of vitality, self-expression, money, positive relationships, health, dysfunctional marriages and families, absence of ambition, and continuous complaints about how things are.

PDD is not the same as clinical depression. Depression is also accompanied by a loss of the experience of possibility. However, PDD does not necessarily imply a loss of one's ability to cope, earn a living, or function in daily life or corporate operations. PDD is a loss of future focus, inspiration, and the ability to create new possibilities for one's self and others.

PDD is a major cause of the lack of innovation in corporations and national competitiveness. Successful innovation is the basis of competitive success in business, government, and life itself. There is an inverse relationship between the inability to create and sustain new possibilities and the ability to invent and sustain innovation. Curiously, because of PDD, corporations, and individuals do not identify the lack of possibility as the root of their recurring challenges, problems, and lack of creativity. The very condition precludes them from becoming aware of the fact that the lack of possibility is the root of the problem. It is a transparent double bind.

PDD is reinforced by media, politicians, and corporate leaders, whose economic or political interests are enhanced by inducing and maintaining fear in their constituencies. Fear is the killer of possibility and possibility thinking. Scared people do what they are told. Therefore, PDD is not simply a matter of psychology and human nature. It is equally a matter of values and the character of leaders.

PDD also, not obviously, helps keep the people in power in power. Either by intention or inadvertently, PDD serves people who control the most valued resources in corporations and government agencies—to have their people not experience too much possibility prevents 'rocking the boat' and changes in the balance of power. The modern Zeitgeist Movement suggests that the pervasive interest-based banking and financial system is a primary source of PDD.

PDD can be a temporary event caused by difficulties. It can also become an addiction in itself. The addiction falls into several classes, each with the power of a monastic order. These include the following:

- Order of the Devout Victim,
- Order of Diminished Delight
- Order of Perpetual Confession
- Order of Incessant Explanation
- Order of Insincere Apology
- Order of Insincere Offers
- Order of Fearful Inaction
- Order of Having to Make a Difference
- Order of Having to Make No difference
- Order of Self Deprecation
- Order of Too Much to Do
- Order of Continual Tidiness
- Order of Perpetually Trite Response
- Order of the Immaculate Inquiry
- Order of Having to Have More
- Order of Nobody Tells Me What to Do
- Order of Committed Inattention
- Order of Desperately Seeking Salvation
- Order of Perfection and Worry
- Order of Terminal Service
- Order of Pathetic Objectives
- Order of Having to Do What You Don't Want To Do
- Order of Unworthy Existence

Everyone suffers from PDD in some areas of their work, community, and personal lives. The very act of naming PDD is a breakthrough for many. Prior to identifying PDD for oneself or one's organization, it's hard to know that Possibility is missing. For some, the addiction is too strong for them to act on the insight. Others, in the moment of seeing that they have been incapable of doing it, immediately begin to identify or invent possibilities.

PDD is a pervasive disorder. War, persistent animosity, and the unwillingness to risk maintain a vicious circle of past-based behavior. At a recent Innovation conference in Shanghai, one Global IT executive discussed broadly-based research showing that 90 percent of companies did not sustain innovation, and 75 percent of new product developments fail. Over 50 percent of acquisitions and more than 50 percent of partnerships either fail or don't live up to expectations.

Identity and possibility have an inverse relationship – the stronger the one, the weaker the other. Fear of loss of identity kills new possibilities. People will give up success, relationships, and sometimes life itself for the preservation of identity. Consider suicide bombers, killing themselves for who they consider themselves to be. On a planetary level, identity is the greatest threat to the survival of humanity as a whole. It is the basis of PDD at local and global levels. Most people and nations appear to be stuck with it.

PDD emerges from the complex culture or identity of the individual, corporation, or nation. This implies that the introduction of "Possibility" as a phenomenon in a culture or within an identity is the only way to deal reliably with PDD. Further, treatment of symptoms, while sometimes necessary, is fruitless over the long term. Since entities have survived successfully within the identity or culture they already have, they are unwilling, except in crisis, to change it. Normally after a crisis, they revert to their prior expressions of PDD.

Therein lies the challenge.

Symptom Checker—Adult PDD Symptoms
- Personal or group identity is the basis of all decisions and behavior
- Need to be right
- Feel like a victim
- Feel spiteful
- Excessive compliance
- Unable to flow with other people or situations
- Unable to inspire others to what they are capable of
- Unable to listen or pay attention to anything inconsistent with what is already known
- Placing the cause of things outside oneself
- Resignation
- Require certainty
- Weak relationships
- Conflicts do not resolve

Corporate PDD Symptoms
- Senior management knows best
- Senior people and bottom people communicate mostly through middle management
- Conviction that we already know
- Reality is physical
- Arbitrary exercise of power
- Shallow relationships
- Lack of inquiry
- Pattern of proceeding to solutions before agreeing on problems
- Lack of innovation
- Innovations do not sustain
- Language disguises underlying realities
- Absence of listening
- Absence of free speech in practice.

FEAR IS THE MIND KILLER

*"Cowards die many times before their death.
The valiant taste of death but once. It seems to me most strange that men should fear, seeing that death, a necessary end…, will come when it will come."*

William Shakespeare, Julius Caesar

Choose something you are afraid of. In my life, I have learned to ask what I am afraid of in a situation or with a person and then do it. This almost always turns out well.

*"I must not fear. Fear is the mind-killer.
Fear is a little death that brings total obliteration.
I will face my fear. I will permit it to pass over me and through me. And when it has gone past, I will turn the inner eye to see its path. Where the fear has gone, there will be nothing.
Only I will remain."*

Frank Herbert, Dune

COMMITMENT TO RADICAL TRANSFORMATION: THE GENIUS OF FERNANDO FLORES

Dr. Fernando Flores is the father of Ontological Coaching. He is recognized as a leader in the world of business process design, coaching, innovation, cognition, and education. His work laid the foundation for much of the current understanding of action workflow and commitment management theory.

Flores spearheaded the new science of organizational transformation based on the idea that conscious, engaged use of language creates reality. It is worth noting that the ways to manage people in a paradigm of committed actions are not the same as the rules employed to manage material and information processes, and to apply a set of rules in one realm to another realm is likely to be a mistake, unworkable and a recipe for getting into trouble.

The commitment paradigm is built on the foundation of pluralism and holism of numerous worlds or sub-worlds evoked by pluralistic cultural traditions, with each set of practices/worlds/sub-worlds offering a different set of possibilities. Flores taught that a set of distinctions live in the language we use. Conversations for change proceed using offers, requests, and committed promises and are augmented by declarations, assertions, and assessments. Four kinds of actions are available in Flores' "conversations for action" model.

1. Commitment

> "Until one is committed, there is hesitancy, the chance to draw back, ineffectiveness. Concerning all acts of initiative and creation, there is one elementary truth, the ignorance of which kills countless ideas and splendid plans: that the moment one definitely commits oneself, then providence moves too. All sorts of things occur to help one that would never otherwise have occurred. A whole stream of events issues from the decision, raising in one's favor all manner of unforeseen incidents and meetings and material assistance, which no man could have dreamt would have come his way."

> William H. Murray, Mount Everest Expedition, 1951

I never heard the word 'commitment' until I was 45 years old. Commitment is the state or quality of being dedicated to a cause, activity, or other people. It is a pledge, a promise, an obligation that restricts freedom of action. Commitment focuses attention. I came to see the world in a new way and was focused and energized as never before. Before that, in school, with family and friends, it was just them and me talking, and what happened next just happened.

2. What's Missing?

> "What's missing anywhere is not there until you ask a question..., and suddenly it appears..., and seems like it was always there but unseen."

At first, it is hard to talk to someone about what is missing because it is not there. We are trained to look for what is actually there because we can then do something useful. The problem with talking about what is missing is that it is not visible. Looking for what is missing is an acquired taste, a practice. It is looking for what is not there, which, if it were there, would make a big difference.

A husband and wife did not care about what the other one cared about. They argued all the time. What was missing was that what she cared about and what he cared about could be important contributions to each other, but they could not see it.

A counselor in a hospital was coaching an assistant on how to be more effective. She had no attention or consideration for what the employee felt or thought. She was concerned with improvements in behavior and attitude without actual conversations that would matter. All of what might have made a difference was missing, absent, not there.

We are hard-wired to see what is there when the answer is often in what is missing and not visible. Noticing what is potentially important but not visible is a skill and a practice that opens a world of opportunity.

3. What's Missing that Gets What's Missing to be Missing?

"We shall not cease from exploration, and at the end of all our exploring will be to arrive where we started and know the place for the first time."

T.S. Eliot, Four Quartets

The Deep Dive is a "Never-Ending Search for what is missing that gets what is missing to be missing." This reveals what lies beneath, the true context or basis that enables or that prevents the resolution of underlying problems.

Consider that in business, government, and much formal education (and in the absence of education), we ignore and suppress the underlying context. This can come from commercial, religious, political, hierarchical control, or self-important reasons. For example, in education, there are three possible realities:

1. Context: The circumstances that form the setting for an event.
2. Action/Process: A series of actions taken in order to achieve a particular end.
3. Result: A consequence, effect, or outcome of something.

The deepest truth is that "Context is Decisive." This determines the circumstances that determine the setting for an event, statement, idea, or terms from which it can be fully understood.

In the United States and elsewhere, where have we recognized benefits but not costs to democracy, many people, and social justice?

- We accepted that money is too often more important than people.
- We accepted authoritarianism culturally as legitimate in leaders and governance.
- We organized what Jesus, the Hebrew prophets, and Buddha taught us.
- We organized the Declaration of Independence to fit our religious beliefs.
- We accepted men's right to be in charge.
- We accepted corporations as having human rights.

- We accepted the primacy of linear thinking and speaking in language and culture.
- We accepted Sovereignty on Earth as God's word.
- We legitimized the right of uninformed people to vote.

Also, with particular respect to the suppression of democracy, the following have become true:

- Concentration of wealth and power
- Free pursuit of self-interest in power and position; power in the hands of the wealthy.
- Corporate and social systems are set up to prevent democracy.
- Reduce democracy so the poor will not take away property.
- Limiting women's and minority rights.
- Business control society by using economic power.
- Corporate business is considered the core national interest.
- Shift society from production to financial and speculative activity—General Electric is 50 percent a financial organization.
- Promotion that "Anti-American" is a totalitarian, authoritarian notion.
- As the economy became global, the needs of the American public became of lesser consequence.
- Tax burden of the wealthy increased for the general public.
- Attacks on social security are driven by the wealthy.
- Government bails out business, but the wealthiest become "too big to fail."

- Organized labor was turned into the enemy because it can be a force for democracy
- Trap people into being consumers, making non-rational choices.
- Public policy discussion is minimal and often unrelated to political party interests.

4. Committed Speaking

"Specific words used in conversations actively empower being responsible and able to honor your word."

Fernando Flores, Committed Action

Declaration: Speaking that is self-evident, needs no support or evidence, reasons why explanations, or proof. Authority comes from the legitimacy of the speaker.

Request: Conversations to enlist the assistance of another in satisfying an underlying concern.

Promise: Speaking to indicate an oath, often invoking a witness, regarding one's future action or behavior.

Assessment: A value judgment, opinion, or explanation in the interest of taking some action, for which you are willing to provide supportive evidence.

"The thought manifests as the word;
The word manifests as the deed;
The deed develops into habit;
And the habit hardens into character;
So watch the thoughts and their ways with care;
And let it spring from love
Born of concern for all beings.
As the shadow follows the body,
As we think, so we become."

— Dhammapada

OBLIQUE SHAFTS OF ILLUMINATION

Transformational magic comes from surprise and confusion, pulling the rug from under what someone already thinks.

Years ago, I was working for a man named Alan Arnott at Perkins Engines in England. He led a manufacturing group concerned about a challenging business problem. Everybody was talking, talking, talking and often never came to the point.

One day, I said something, and one of the people stood up and asked Alan, *"Why do you hire this guy?"*

Alan said, quickly and directly, *"He's always bringing oblique shafts of illumination. You don't know where it comes from or even what it's about, but it lights up the room. It lights up possibilities that weren't there before he spoke. Some are oblique, some come right through the window, but they light up the situation."*

Some people got it right away, and we went on with the meeting. When I became a student in the Gestalt Institute in Cleveland's psychology\philosophy certification program, the headteacher was Erving Polster, who is now 100 years old. He's an extraordinary gentleman, a genius, and a deep, deep thinker. At a point, I realized he never does what you think he's going to do.

I once asked him, *"What is God?"*

He said, *"God is the perfect integration of poetry, emotion, and ideas."*

I've lived my whole life with that idea. Erving is always saying something that has two or three parts that make you think something you didn't already think. And I noticed that I was doing that much of the time. I was imitating him without knowing it. I was proud of that and just turned it loose. It had become automatic.

I then began to notice that this behavior on my part was driving some clients away! They started out loving who I am and what I do, but over time I was making them uncomfortable. They wanted to make cars or jam or applesauce, and I was creating thoughts they could not share. These thoughts would help them tremendously, and when they were in pain, confused, or stuck at the beginning, they saw the benefit. Though when things got stable and practical, they didn't want to do it anymore.

So, I'd move from client to client. It would start out with an amazing impact, but then when they saw that what they had was off the reservation, they wanted to do what was normal, and I wasn't providing enough certainty. They didn't want the endless deep dives into the nature of their reality. They wanted to make money, sell whatever they were selling, and not rock the boat. I endlessly wanted deep dives. So...while an oblique shaft of illumination brings insight, new futures, and deep thinking, people don't want it when they've got a house to clean or whatever it is that they consider essential.

I once knew a brilliant counselor who had a near-death experience, and from that started to trust her immediate experience completely...and ignore the rest. From this, she became an unbelievably effective counselor and observer of what a person needs to transform a situation.

I asked her, *"If you want to transform a whole company or a whole group, what do you do?"*

She said, *"You ask the leaders what kinds of energy they avoid. Where won't they go? What are they not like? And you train them and train them, so they become able, if not to embrace, to at least deal with and operate from energies they typically avoid."*

Oblique Shafts of Illumination **are** a moment-to-moment reality. Reality is a moment. When it becomes a principle, reality can get flakier and flakier. Therapy, making things better, is always the opposite. If you talk too much, the reality that transforms is to not talk so much.

Experience is what transforms. Most people will not allow themselves to have experiences that their church doesn't like, that their family doesn't like, that their wife doesn't like. The obliqueness comes from not being stuck with what you already think. You can't think from angles. It tends to happen the way it usually does.

I've been doing this wonderful Zen mantra, *"Om mani padre om,"* over and over again. It's miraculous because what happens is that I stop thinking. And when I stop thinking, I'm able to think! I'm able to imagine. I don't know where it comes from or what the source of real thinking is. But most of what we think is not what it is, but just a way of keeping some boss or someone in your life and past happy.

I sometimes get in trouble with language, from words. As soon as you think you are the words, you're stuck in linear subject-object time. As soon as you start to explain, you've lost access to possibility.

Transformation is in the experience. "I love you" is an experience. If I tell you all the ways, I love you, how I love you, why I love you, what stops me from loving you, the magic, by degrees, goes away. Life is not a linguistic event. Life is a vibrational body event. The more you organize it, the more the experience gets forced into what's possible from the language. Often, what's transformational is when there is very little or no explanation, but more from an unusual experience and not knowing.

POSSIBILITIES

"There are thousands of channels in our consciousness; it is up to us to choose the channel."
                                                                Thich Nhat Hanh

There are countless possibilities in the universe that only become real when you ask a question. In so many companies, governments, and relationships, there are many forbidden questions and forbidden statements. Almost everyone knows what you never say to your boss or your wife or your customer.

I am conscious of many things that I never say. Often, what I say draws upon consciousness in service of some motive or desire I've got. It seems to me that consciousness itself is a major source of potential futures, better relationships, and a better world.

I woke up one night at 3 o'clock in the morning, dwelling on a book I had read called God is Consciousness Without an Object. I said to myself, if God is everything, and is consciousness without an object, then I too am part of everything and also must be myself "Consciousness Without an Object." This made little sense in everyday conversation, but I asked myself the question, *"If I am consciousness without an object, what is possible?"*

I then asked myself questions, assuming I was in Zero Gravity and surrounded by Nothingness. Some of what I then said to myself made a little sense, and some were remarkably novel, interesting, and possible. Somehow, starting from nothing, from Zero, and so on, led to new insight.

Wow! A new game in town! From considering I was consciousness without an object came the following:

- I spent a number of moments conscious about nothing but consciousness.
- Filled in instantly with love.
- Prospects of life and death.
- Years of memoried events.
- Possibility alone with itself.
- Nazis, morons, uneducated, cruel, careless, unkind, thoughtless, money is God.
- Conscious, awake, in the moment so quick it's gone.
- No content; awake without an object anywhere.
- Inspirations of joy and fear.

Advanced Freedom is Consciousness without an Object. Our own sense of self-importance assures us that the impossible does not become possible.

DAGAZ

It is an energy field that lets you see and think without being stuck in the past, without needing or being stuck in the future, and with the magic of the present moment. "Dagaz" is a symbol of a "rune" used by Germanic peoples from about the 3rd to the 13th century.

The 'point of poise' entails balancing polarities so that all mystery is revealed to consciousness. The transformation of paradox into non-dual awareness occurs with Dagaz energies. It is to find the center between two extremes and maintain a state of mind undisturbed by any mental or emotional storm. At the center, all power is to be found, and equilibrium is desirable attainment.

This practice eventually leads to the practitioner no longer requiring a single right or wrong answer to the mysteries, and many truths can exist complementary to one another. No one single belief or viewpoint is sufficient, and so all beliefs and viewpoints can be progressively abandoned. In the stillness and silent questioning of the mind that is left behind, all truth resounds.

Dagaz can be used to gain absolute stillness. It is invisible, transforming power. The vibrational patterns of the self or an object can be dampened so that the perception of material things to the human eye grows faint. Finding this point of poise takes great skill and practice with Dagaz, but mastery of this rune of enlightenment leads down the path of disappearance. Mastery of invisibility leads to the understanding of existence through its opposite: non-existence.

- The left-hand side is the past.
- The right-hand side is the future.
- The center point is *emptiness*, zero gravity, the place where a new future, Real Thinking, Escape Velocity, and Collaborative innovation can begin.

THE POWER OF US

Sometimes I think the most important question to keep asking is, *"Who am I?"* What if reality was actually the Power of Us, and the Power of Me separately was an illusion, brain-driven, cultural-driven? What if there is only one thing going on, and we are part of it?

Immediately, I imagine voices accusing me of being a communist, taking people's money, things, and freedom, and the enemy of democratic people everywhere. Or maybe the Power of Us and the Power of Me are like the front of the hand and the back of the hand, both real and brother and sister, whether do you like it or not?

What if reality, what's really real, consists of what it's like for you, what it's like for me, what it's like for us, what it's like for a universe we can't understand? That suggests that what's really going on is everything and the best we can do is to pay attention to what we love with no arrogance.

Most of us come to believe that our own reality is more real than others. This means that countless people are living in important ways in different realities:

- "My Reality"
- "Your Reality"
- "Our Reality"
- "Other's Reality"
- "Reality That the Whole Is Always Greater Than the Sum of Its Parts"

We have it in us to tell each other what's real for us, deeply and factually true, in honest, gentle ways that allow each of us to make peace and possibly build bridges with others. Short of that, as individuals and as a human race, we are doomed to divisiveness, doom, and eternal little and big wars.

Identity is the identity of *"Us,"* the consciousness of *"Us,"* and an element of Conscious Leadership more powerful than *"me and* you" or *"me or* you." When people feel the certainty that *"We are in this together,"* a positive future becomes even more possible.

>(This insight is stimulated by the remarkable work of Alexander Berlonghi in coaching and the improvement of human affairs.)

THE TALKING STICK

Traditionally, the Talking Stick is a tool used by many indigenous people when they meet in council or a group. The person holding the stick speaks about what is deeply true for them right now and what they are aware of in the present moment. Everyone else is asked to listen. When finished, the speaker passes the stick.

Most often, the practice of the Talking Stick provides the missing link to go beyond where people have stalled in Collaborative Innovation; in groups or business, in situations where people feel stuck in seemingly unsolvable circumstances, in abrasive conflicts, or where life and its essence—relationships—feel flat and featureless.

In recent times, we have been using glass art versions of the talking stick that combine the power, rich symbolism, and ancient wisdom of indigenous people with the color, beauty, mystery, strength, and fragility of blown glass and magical flow.

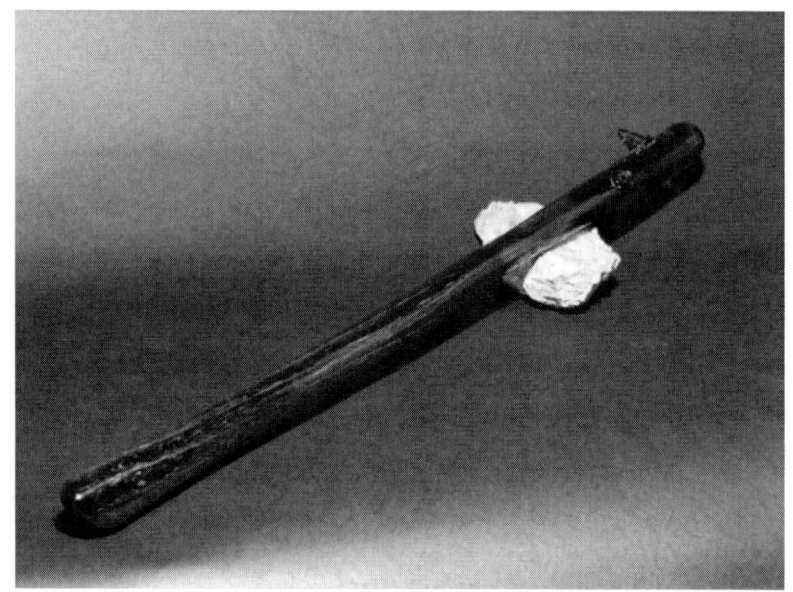

G. Michael Smith, http://www.thecreativityunleashed.com/

Robert Barthelemy, Ph.D. says in *Speak from the Soul, Hear from the Heart,* "Picture these situations:

— The leaders of five European nations that are in the process of destroying each other have to begin a conversation that might lead to a workable peace process.

— The CEOs of ten of the biggest corporations in America have to agree to an approach that will merge these ten independent companies into three mega-companies.

— A Four-Star General and a politically-appointed Service Secretary have to construct a process that will define the future readiness of the United States Air Force."

The common element in all of these situations was a simple but beautiful Talking Stick, handcrafted for me by my friend, Ross LewAllen, a Santa Fe shaman, jeweler, and artist. Ross spent over a month creating my Talking Stick and carved a variety of unique symbols and jewels into it. One of them, a Silver Eagle, represented what he believed was my Origin as well as my Destiny.

When he presented me with the Talking Stick, he told me that there were only two rules in its use: whoever holds the Talking Stick must Speak from the Soul, and whoever is listening must Hear from the Heart.

While it is simply an attractive piece of art, it has been magical. I began using it in my work, and it always led to meaningful conversations that quickly got to the heart of the matter. At first, my friends and colleagues were surprised that a nuclear rocket scientist who spent his life trying to make a difference in a giant military bureaucracy would believe in such a thing. But Talking Sticks have been used for thousands of years when conscious, meaningful conversations were required.

The rules seem simple, but they are often very difficult to follow. *Speaking from the Soul, Hearing from the Heart* may be the only way to get beyond our busy little brains and all of the sensory inputs that get in the way of having Conscious Conversations.

And yes, with assistance from my Talking Stick, the leaders did find a way to start the Dayton Peace Process, the CEOs did create the three biggest aerospace companies on the globe, and the United States Air Force remains the most powerful military deterrent in the world.

DIALOGUE

Dialogue is a conversation. It is not a debate. The goal is not to win or lose. The goal is to find shared meaning. Dialogue takes time. It often needs to keep going for days, weeks, or months. Dialogue is not competitive. It is a discipline, practice. Dialogue is not possible in a competitive environment. It is possible in competitive environments to bracket the competition for as long as it takes to have a shared conversation that brings insight and hope to a situation.

When hunter-gatherer bands met together, they had no apparent agenda nor any predetermined purpose. Such gatherings seemed to provide and reinforce a kind of cohesive bond or fellowship that allowed its participants to know what was required of them without the need for instruction or much further verbal interchange. Dialogue is a situation where we suspend our opinions and judgments in order to be able to listen to each other.

Dialogue is a collective inquiry—not only into the content of what each of us says, thinks, and feels but also into the underlying motivations, assumptions, and beliefs that lead us to do so.

> *"Without dialogue, every intractable problem stays that way."*
>
> David Bohm

CONNECT AND MOVE ON

I discovered with my friend Tony that real thinking requires the ability to connect and move on. We're fluid and are able to connect, make contact, touch, and always move on. In the absence of that ability, you can't do real thinking but get stuck with what you've already got.

I asked my son, Michael, what makes his glass art great, and he said it's when he's able to reach the paradox between the perfect integration between intention and flow. He knows what he wants to create, but he flows.

I once saw him swinging a ball of hot glass through the air; scary, hot, on fire. He was very intentional but also entirely in flow, and he was balancing his attention between those points. You can't have real thinking unless there's both flow and intention.

THERE IS NO SECRET INGREDIENT…ONLY YOU

King Fu Panda

"When you think you already know something - that is the most perfect barrier against learning."

Frank Herbert

Ultimately and usually, I find out that nobody, no good idea, no stroke of good fortune, is going to pull my fat out of the fire. A client in England once said that you have to control your own business. The paradox (a seemingly absurd or self-contradictory statement or proposition that, when investigated or explained, may prove to be well-founded or true) is that even when there is harmony, it still has to feel possible that you're controlling your own business.

So very often, I expect that a new relationship, a new partnership, and a new opportunity will assure, facilitate, and guarantee continuing success. It just isn't true. As soon as I lose sight of my awareness of the fact that there is no secret ingredient, that ultimately, it's just me, even during the times when it's me and others, I become overly dependent, less than fully responsible, upset that others are not doing what I want, and often want to start again elsewhere with someone that will agree with me.

A vicious circle.

- What's missing that gets what's missing to be missing?
- What's not possible, which, if it were possible, would make a big difference?
- What..., if only I could?
- What must I have an agreement to, the lack of which suppresses my freedom?
- In this extraordinary moment, what is the most important thing to focus on?
- What's the awful truth?
- "A paradox is not a problem." *David Bohm*
- "For performance aspirations beyond normal, commitment, *not reason,* does the sorting." *Michael Reid*

CHARACTER IS DECISIVE

"If you apply yourself to the task before you, following the right reason calmly, seriously, vigorously, calmly, allowing nothing else to distract you, but keeping your divine part pure, as if you might be bound to give it back immediately; if you hold this, expecting nothing fearing nothing, but satisfied with your present activities according to nature, and with heroic truth in every word and sound which you utter, you will live happily. And there is no man who is able to prevent this."

Marcus Aurelius

I've come to believe that in business and in life, character is decisive. Eventually, a person's character becomes the Captain of His or Her Ship, with the combination of mental characteristics and behavior
that distinguish and predict their behavior.

Many People are:

- Successful
- Thoughtful
- Care for their troops
- Courageous
- Competent
- Creative
- Do not lie
- Fair
- Direct
- Honest
- Imaginative
- Supportive

I worked for years as an Organizational Behavior consultant to a major consumer goods corporation. At one point, they were going to promote someone to be president. Both the two candidates were competent, attractive, creative, and successful in the business. Both were committed to profit and high performance. One also had a particular concern for the well-being of people in the company. They promoted the one with a deeper concern for profit. I thought that this promotion reflected the true values of the company.

No one I heard of ever wrote a love song or a poem about a corporation. I'm convinced that no man or woman with a commitment to money over the well-being of people should be promoted to senior positions in business, government, or healthcare.

UNCHARACTERISTIC RESULTS REQUIRE UNCHARACTERISTIC ACTION

The National Peace Academy Campaign was the vision of a man named Bryant Wedge. The dream was to create a national academy at the level of West Point, Annapolis, and the U.S. Air Force, devoted to research, practice, and action in the areas of non-violent dispute resolution in the United States and around the world. The idea was to create a national ethic of waging peace with equal conviction to our capacity for violence and war. There were critical challenges in managing volunteers, relating to and negotiating with members of Congress, lack of money, and continuing resistance from the Defence Departments, Schools of Foreign Service, Arms Manufacturers, certain media, and many members of Congress. On the one hand, it seemed like Don Quixote tilting at windmills, and on the other hand, a noble, worthwhile and committed purpose with leaders who really meant it.

The original mission was to have the U.S. Congress create a commission to study the viability and merits of such an effort. The National Peace Academy Campaign was a low budget, largely volunteer effort to enable this. My role was to help build teams and coach and counsel leaders in breakthrough thinking and creative ways to engage in constructive conflict resolution. Our deeper role was to act as a "conscience" for all of them to bring together the ethics of their values and the power politics and opposition that would naturally come from the Defense Department, schools of foreign service, media, and certain members of the Congress.

In fact, the commission bill was passed with a $500,000 grant, and after a year of negotiation, forward movement, and sacrifice of some of the original principles, Congress passed a bill to create the National Institute of Peace, which now resides in a beautiful building located on the Washington Mall. They deal with extensive world conflict resolution research and facilitation. We did not accomplish the vision, and it was a strong step in the right direction.

<u>Political Will: Bending the Arc of History</u>
William J Spencer

PERFORMANCE AND SOCIETAL BREAKTHROUGHS THAT EXPLODE CULTURAL LIMITS ON WHAT'S POSSIBLE

- Don't do a lot of explaining
- Know that people are as important as money
- Know that energy vampires exist. Energy vampires force others into transactions, irrelevant conversations, and the absence of helpful silence
- Energy vampires prevent others from experiencing the open space between us and places where you can have mutual collaboration and radical curiosity
- Be silent and listen
- Avoid noise
- Do not use force but use power, the ability to bring something into existence that people want and are sustainable
- Generate, manage and stay connected with people to sustain and expand vibrational energy in and between people
- Avoid transaction
- Un-conceal the existing condition and create a new contract
- Allow for nothingness; let there be open space for people to create their own material
- Consider "betterment" as if it were a gene in your body, a constant necessity. Remember that a good idea is only good at all levels of context, process, and result. If an idea is only good at the level of context or process, or result, it is not a good idea. A transformative leader assures that context, process, and the result are all attended to with conviction

- There is a brother-sister relationship between betterment and curiosity. No curiosity, no change
- Create games for people to play with more and more consciousness and enlightenment
- Curiosity, radical curiosity squared, is what creates energy
- Intention moves something along purpose lines. If you do anything else, you stop the flow and stop the magic

JOSEPH CAMPBELL AND THE TRANSFORMATIONAL POWER OF MYTHOLOGY

Joseph Campbell was a brilliant Mythologist and Teacher. He said, *"Myths are stories that are based on tradition. Some may have factual origins, while others are completely fictional. But myths are more than mere stories and serve an even more profound purpose in ancient and modern cultures. Myths are sacred tales that explain the world and man's experience."*

Campbell also said that *"The first function of mythology is to evoke in the individual a sense of grateful, affirmative awe before the monstrous mystery that is existence."*

The second function of mythology is to present an image of the cosmos, an image of the universe round about, that will maintain and elicit this experience of awe, [or]... to present an image of the cosmos that will maintain your sense of mystical awe and explain everything that you come into contact within the universe around you.

The third function of a mythological order is to validate and maintain a certain sociological system: a shared set of rights and wrongs, proprieties or improprieties, on which your particular social unit depends for its existence.

The fourth function of myth is psychological. That myth must carry the individual through the stages of his life, from birth through maturity, through senility to death. The mythology must do so in accord with the social order of his group, the cosmos as understood by his group, and monstrous mystery.

==============================
GRATITUDE VIDEO

This video will show the real impact of gratitude and its implication in our lives:

http://consciouslifenews.com/beautiful-video-gratitude-louie-schwartzberg-tedxsf/112362

==============================

HUNA SCIENCE © Serge Kahili King

The science now called Huna is a very old Hawaiian science. Some believe that it may be as old as 35,000 years old and is a part of the original teachings of the peoples of the earth, which were centered here in Hawaii on a continent that now no longer exists. All that remains physically of that land are the mountain peaks of the island chain called Hawaii. Long after the original teachings of the peoples of the earth were codified and spread out all over the world, the continent disappeared. The teachings continued in Hawaii and in other parts of the world.

For a long time prior to 750 A.D., there flourished a system of personal development, healing, and spiritual discipline that was known by "everyone." The system was a balanced system—one that honored men and women equally. There were almost no secrets; in fact, there were so few secrets that the information that comprised the techniques wasn't even organized or formally taught. It just formed the background of "how it was" in the world.

In the Huna tradition, there are seven basic principles that govern life and the creation of existence. They are condensed into seven Hawaiian words. They aren't easily translated into the English language, so it's best to use a sentence describing the essence of each word.

(1) IKE—The World Is What You Think It Is. When one is aware of their thoughts, words, and actions in nearly every moment throughout their day, one can, after a period of time, by choosing a more positive, peaceful, loving, and compassionate way of being, find that the path that they are on soon becomes nothing but positive, peaceful, loving and compassionate.

(2) KALA—There Are No Limits. There are no limits in this universe. If we fully understand and believe this, the only thing on this 3-dimensional earth plane that has limits is our own mind, nine times out of ten due to conditioning from society and our upbringing.

(3) MAKIA—Energy Goes Where Attention Goes. Put all your energy into achieving what you want out of this life; be focused and clear on what it really is you want. Place your energy into having a happy, joyful, and loving life now.

(4) MANAWA—Now Is the Moment of Power. Especially in today's world, we all tend to be living either in the past or in the future and are certainly not in the present moment. When you're either in the past or future, your energy becomes scattered and drained.

(5) ALOHA—To Love Is to Be Happy With. ALOHA—the real meaning of this word is ALO = to be with, to share an experience, to be in the moment. OHA = joy, happiness. HA = life, breath, spirit. To love is to share the happiness of life here and now. This really sums everything up, and that is love.

(6) MANA—All Power Comes from Within. True power that is from the heart and not from the ego is essential to achieving your goals.

(7) PONO—Effectiveness Is The Measure Of Truth. It's all about attitude and having a positive outlook on life. Try and be positive as much as possible, and before you know it, everything in your life will become positive.

THE MERLIN FACTOR: THINKING FROM THE FUTURE

Legend has it that Merlin, the Magician, was the great King Arthur's mentor. As depicted in *The Once and Future King* by T.H. White, Merlin had an uncanny ability to know the future. White's legend provides an apt metaphor for a 'future-first' perspective that successfully instills strategic intent in organizations and their people. He would occasionally give Arthur some insight into just how he knew what was going to happen before it did:

"Ah yes," Merlin said. "How did I know to set breakfast for two?... Now ordinary people are born forwards in Time, if you understand what I mean, and nearly everything in the world goes forward too. This makes it quite easy for ordinary people to live... But unfortunately, I was born at the wrong end of time, and I have to live backward from in front, while surrounded by a lot of people living forward from behind..."

The Merlin Factor is a way of living in the world and the ability to think from the point of view of the future. It is the ability to enlist people as Ambassadors who listen, speak, and act on behalf of that future and become committed to performance breakthroughs that explode existing cultural limits on what's possible.

The premise is that the principal impediment to changing an organization's strategic direction is its existing culture: that is, people's current beliefs about the limits of what is possible. Changing people's beliefs about the future can produce extraordinary improvements in relationships, quality management, technical innovation, customer service, and profitability. Exceptional leaders cultivate the Merlin-like habit of acting in the present moment as ambassadors of a radically different future in order to imbue their organizations and people with a breakthrough vision of what it is possible to achieve.

- Do something you are afraid of and watch something wonderful happen.
- Until you get to a root cause, keep asking, if not for what basic cause this performance problem could be eliminated?
- Make one unreasonable request.
- If you knew you could not fail, what would you do?
- What breakthrough in the Future you will you commit to?
- What is your favorite way of playing small?
- What is your true purpose in life?
- What true commitments are being thwarted?
- Why should I listen to you?
- Where are you grasping?
- What is working well around here?
- What is your request for coaching?
- What are you aware of?
- What stops you from listening?
- Are you listening to the little wise voice in your head?

THE MERLIN FACTOR: AVALON AND GLASTONBURY

In the Legend of King Arthur, Glastonbury symbolizes a visible city and Avalon an invisible city. Each, however, occupied the same physical territory. Only a few individuals like Merlin, the King's Counsel, knew how to find their way between the two. In fact, most people no longer even knew of Avalon's existence, let alone how to get there.

By analogy, each of today's corporations, government agencies, and communities includes these same two dimensions. In a corporation's visible Glastonbury are found familiar objects and events such as buildings, machines, materials, products, services, vendors, customers, and stock prices. Also, there, unfortunately, often reside a host of problems.

In the same companies' invisible Avalon are relational qualities such as mutual trust, honesty, compassionate listening, forgiveness and reconciliation, caring relationships, cooperation toward grand visions, confidence in the future, alignment among personnel, and commitment to others' success. Avalon, too, harbors difficulties. Both dimensions have their own cultures and structures, forms of energy, and outputs.

Both Glastonbury and Avalon are essential to the vibrant health, genuine success, and continuous improvement of any organization. Glastonbury deals primarily with objective reality—things tangible and countable. Avalon is most concerned with relational realities. Without Avalon, it lacks heart and kindness and the vital experience of Mutuality.

THE "CALLING:" ENERGY THAT EMBRACES

Bridge over the River Awe, near Oban, Scotland

Rumi said, "*Be silently drawn by the strange pull of what they really love.*"

'The Calling' is the transformational bridge between past and future, ancient wisdom into the modern world.

The approach seems to follow their own invention, special to them, which is an assemblage point, their unique way of organizing reality, that's immediately recognized by almost anyone and instantly pulls the rug out from under what they already think.

In our attempt to help people become 'Masters' by enabling their own approach to Collaborative Innovation. I'm reminded of when I asked my cousin Warren, a self-made billionaire, "*How do I turn my business from a personal art form to a successful business?*"

Right away, he said, "*Find someone who is already successful at what you want and copy what they do.*"

Here then is a collection of Masters who have had the greatest impact on my work and life and the pervasive singular framework for the lesson and impact they had on me and others I've touched. I offer these as practical practices and commitments for becoming or enhancing your own Mastery in Collaborative Innovation.

ZOE MARAE: *"I am a scientist who believes in vibrational magic." Zoe is a genius who worked at Harvard in science research. She had a near-death experience, after which she started trusting only her 'present' moment experience. She was the most amazing counselor and scientist in the area of personal growth, energy expansion, and making betterment happen.*

She said that "Vibration is a consciousness that goes to our core. You and I have it. I feel it. It's a higher-order, that vibration, based in a vibrational spirit which completes our old experience of being separate, of being different, and moving beyond that resistance and control to vibrational flow."

Zoe said that "In the presence of vibrational energy, wonder, awe, inspiration, mystery, and inexplicable wholeness, anything becomes possible."

ERVING POLSTER: Oblique Shafts of Illumination—*"I pay attention to my confusion before my certainty."*

ALBERT EINSTEIN: *"I'm not smarter than others, just passionately curious."*

EDGAR MITCHELL, Sixth Man on The Moon: *"You develop instant global consciousness, a people orientation, an intense dissatisfaction with the world, and a compulsion to do* something about it. From out there, from the Moon, international politics looks so petty. It's an immediate show of respect, mixed with fear and wonder."

JEFFREY MIRONOV: *"There is only one thing, a singularity embracing everything."*

FRANK HERBERT: *"Fear is the mind-killer."*

MICHAEL SMITH: *"The perfect integration of intention and flow."*

ALEXANDER BERLONGHI: *"Ontology is the study of "being" and the practice of the experience of 'us.'"*

VICTOR SANCHEZ: *"Systems with most available energy will prevail."*

WERNER ERHARD: *"The way things work around here is my way, or they don't work at all."*

BART BARTHELEMY: *"The power of white light"* and *"bounce off the elephant."*

GREY ANTELOPE: *"Look under the rock, and the answer will come to you."*

DAVID NORRIS: *"Transformation is a discipline that solves problems not available from common levels of thinking."*

THICH KNAT HANH: *"Grasping is the source of all suffering."*

RON BYNUM: *"Stay on purpose until the end of the day no matter how you feel."*

TANIA EHMAN: *"Only have one clear message, distilled many times over, crafted with words that touch the heart."*

ROBERT MIRABAL: *"The trees and the lands are your brothers and sisters."*

TONY TURNBULL: *"God is a never-ending inquiry between us and in me."*

MICHAEL REID: *"Transformation begins with distinction."*

WARREN ALPERT: Four questions:

1. *"Who the hell are you?"*
2. *"Why should I listen to you?"*
3. *"How will you get me what I really want?"*
4. *"Who that's really credible in the world will stand for you?"*

LEW EPSTEIN: Every once in a while, you meet someone unlike anyone else you've ever known. Lou Epstein was such a man. He was a master of recognizing how other people were being. If you were sad and didn't realize it, Lou would start to cry. He was kind, honest, funny, and sometimes a regular comedian on stage in everyday conversation. In some ways, he was not of this world. There was no severity in him.

The first time we met, he told me, *"If you never scare a woman, she will do anything you want."* His extreme sensitivity in everyday conversation, in counseling relationships, and in speaking the truth while always kind was a wake-up call.

Lew taught us about Generous Listening with deep compassion for the feelings and aspirations of someone else. I had usually considered myself a tough guy and that being direct, even painful, was easy, the way to be in charge, the way to succeed and protect myself. I learned from Lou how to be kind before being direct, and my business rapidly improved, as did my relationships. Lew died, but his presence is still very much with my wife and me.

HARMONY THROUGH CONFLICT

Harmony through Conflict requires the intent to come to, or return to, alignment or shared commitment. It calls for a background intent to create an experience of 'us'—being *in* something together. This is impossible to define, as opposites must be included. It requires full self-expression and a willingness to fight or engage in getting another's attention, and the capacity/skill to not automatically react to differences.

It's not risk-averse but is willing to forgive and forbear. It's not soft but an insistence on honesty and truth about one's actual experience. It's a search for a metaphor that respects and embraces everyone involved, heals, and avoids right-wrong language in and between people.

- Avoid transaction.
- Un-conceal the existing condition and create a new contract.
- Allow for nothingness; let there be open space for people to create their own material.
- Consider "betterment" as if it were a gene in your body, a constant necessity.
- Remember that a good idea is only good at all levels of context, process, and result. If an idea is only good at the level of context or process, or result, it is not a good idea. A transformative leader assures that context, process, and the result are all attended to with conviction.
- There is a brother-sister relationship between betterment and curiosity. No curiosity, no change.
- Create games for people to play with more and more consciousness and enlightenment.

- Curiosity, radical curiosity squared, is what creates energy.

SUSTAINABILITY

Sustainability is a popular word. It usually means how to take something we like and keep it going. Sadly, the reasons things often stop working are complex and embedded in current circumstances and the ways people have come to operate. Often, there are potentially new ways of operating and thinking that are suppressed by what the culture or leadership allows.

Sustainability is best considered just a word and can mean starting something brand new and better, going back to Ground Zero, Zero Gravity, considering what's missing, and creating a promising, currently non-existent alternative.

Consider that "Now is the moment of power," and yesterday isn't. Starting with what you really want to see in the future and building a bridge back from that future is more apt to stimulate novel practices that can sustain the essence of what it is that you really want to sustain.

COACHABILITY

Coaching is one thing and sounds like a great idea. Coachability is a deep well, and often where a person is not coachable is not obvious. The sad truth is that no coachability means no curiosity, no progress.

Conversations and inquiries into where others are not coachable can lead to great leaps forward in performance and relationship or prove that what's needed is un-coachable or that you are unwilling to go all the way with what is necessary. Sometimes, fear is the showstopper. Sometimes internal self-importance keeps people from seeing clearly. Sometimes the person doesn't feel safe in areas they typically avoid. Sometimes the "space" between you and others is cluttered by pre-existing opinions or unresolved issues. Coachability is an important and deep well and always worthy of attention.

COACHING

I've known many people who asked for or agreed to coach, and I found out that many had their own definition of what it meant. When I started as a Coach, I assumed it would be like high school football, where I was told, *"Run forward six steps turn right, and look for the ball."* I got to think that being a coach in the world of business and relationships would be something like that, and people would follow my instructions. They would listen and do what I wanted.

As it turned out, what often happened was, internally, they said, *"I'll listen and then do what I want,"* or *"I'll follow your coaching, and withdraw, stop, or modify by degrees as I see fit,"* or *"I'll follow your lead until I get scared,"* or *"I'll trust you now, but that's not a guarantee about later,"* or *"I'll be honest with you, and whatever happens, it's okay if it breaks down with circumstances."*

I learned that Coaching in business or in life is like water. You can't tell how deep it is simply by looking at it. I spent years expecting Coaching to be like what I thought it should be and then discovered that much of the time, I needed to be as much in charge of their performance as they were. Over and over, I learned that *"It's all energy, and it's all me."*

Sometimes, Coaching is a slippery slope and requires regular conversation, inquiry, and honesty. Sometimes, the Coaching just works, and it's grand.

THE VALUE OF BEING USELESS

"It is one of the most ingrained and unconsciously pernicious of our psychological habits to treat almost everything we do as a means to an end."

https://tricycle.org/magazine/uselessness/

"The Zen teacher Kodo Sawaki (1880–1965) once asserted that "Zazen is useless." If we truly engage this assertion, we discover that doing this "useless" thing is profoundly different from everything else we do in our lives. It may, in fact, be the only useless thing we ever do.

Our whole lives are organized around one purpose or another. Everything we do has a purpose, whether it's to earn money, have a good time, or do good for others. Everything we do can thus be judged on some scale of accomplishment: How am I doing? There is always an answer, sometimes out to three decimal points. We are so used to everything having a purpose we may even find ourselves asking the question, *"What is the purpose of life itself?"* We'll never find the answer to that one because the question itself makes no sense. We have hopelessly conflated "purpose" with meaning and value.

This is why it can be so hard to answer when our friends or relatives ask us why we practice Zen. The question presumes that Zen is a technique with a purpose, a practice with something as its goal. *"Does it make you calm or happy?"* As in the case of any koan, it doesn't work to answer either yes or no. If zazen is truly useless, the first moment we do it, just as Dogen says, "We have entered into a totally different realm. We are instantaneously off the grid, so to speak, of means and ends, of progress and goals. We are in a whole new world where what we are doing is not, cannot, be justified by something outside of itself, by what it's going to get us, or where it's going to take us. We just sit. We just are."

CARL SAGAN'S BALONEY DETECTION KIT

Based on the book,
*The Demon-Haunted World:
Science as a candle in the dark*

The following are tools for testing arguments and detecting fallacious or fraudulent arguments:

- Wherever possible, there must be independent confirmation of the facts.
- Encourage substantive debate on the evidence by knowledgeable proponents of all points of view.
- Arguments from authority carry little weight (in science, there are no "authorities").
- Spin more than one hypothesis - don't simply run with the first idea that caught your fancy.
- Try not to get overly attached to a hypothesis just because it's yours.
- Quantify wherever possible.
- If there is a chain of argument, every link in the chain must work.
- "Occam's razor"—if there are two hypotheses that explain the data equally well, choose the simpler.
- Ask whether the hypothesis can, at least in principle, be falsified (shown to be false by some unambiguous test). In other words, is it testable? Can others duplicate the experiment and get the same result?

COMMON FALLACIES OF LOGIC AND RHETORIC

- *Ad hominem*—attacking the arguer and not the argument.
- Argument from "authority."
- Argument from adverse consequences (putting pressure on the decision-maker by pointing out dire consequences of an "unfavorable" decision).
- Appeal to ignorance (absence of evidence is not evidence of absence).
- Special pleading (typically referring to God's will).
- Begging the question (assuming an answer in the way the question is phrased).
- Observational selection (counting the hits and forgetting the misses). Statistics of small numbers (such as drawing conclusions from inadequate sample sizes).
- Misunderstanding the nature of statistics (*President Eisenhower expressing astonishment and alarm on discovering that fully half of all Americans have below-average intelligence!*)
- Inconsistency (e.g., military expenditures based on worst case scenarios but scientific projections on environmental dangers thriftily ignored because they are not "proved").
- *Non sequitur*—"it does not follow"—the logic falls down.
- *Post hoc, ergo propter hoc*—"it happened after so it was caused by"—confusion of cause and effect.
- Meaningless question ("What happens when an irresistible force meets an immovable object?).

- Excluded middle—considering only the two extremes in a range of possibilities (making the "other side" look worse than it really is).
- Short-term v. long-term—a subset of excluded middle ("Why pursue fundamental science when we have so huge a budget deficit?").
- Slippery slope—a subset of excluded middle—unwarranted extrapolation of the effects (give an inch, and they will take a mile).
- Confusion of correlation and causation.
- Straw man—caricaturing (or stereotyping) a position to make it easier to attack.
- Suppressed evidence or half-truths.
- Weasel words—for example, use euphemisms for war such as "police action" to get around limitations on Presidential powers. "An important art of politicians is to find new names for institutions which under old names have become odious to the public."

Prepared by Michael Paine
27 January 1998.

CONSIDER: THE WORLD IS WHAT YOU THINK IT IS

Victor Frankl Video:
https://www.youtube.com/watch?v=UgVA6nXCj1U

Inner Worlds—Outer Worlds Video
https://video.search.yahoo.com/yhs/search?fr=yhs-Lkry-F01&hsimp=yhsSF01&hspart=Lkry&p=inner+worlds+outer+worlds+you+tube#id=2&vid=0bdb2ab641d0ce227568a9c77f995baf&action=click

THE COLLABORATIVE ENERGY QUOTIENT (CEQ):
A Self-Directed Assessment Of Your Behavior And Capacity For Collaboration With Others

The CEQ is an assessment tool to increase effectiveness and positive relationship. It is a way of thinking about the future, the past, and the present.

The CEQ reveals how you deal with ordinary or extraordinary situations. It shows your typical behaviors with respect to collaboration. It may demonstrate ways of thinking and behaving that might be improved for the sake of Innovative Collaboration.

Einstein's theory ($E=MC^2$) allowed the splitting of the atom and transformed physical mass into explosive amounts of energy. Such dramatic energy expansion is available in collaboration, in business, government, community, and personal life. As with Einstein's theory, this is subject to testing, and it can be a vehicle for understanding and affecting Innovative Collaboration in projects and relationships.

Our version of **$E=MC^2$** is based on four principles:

1. Systems and people with the most available energy will prevail.
2. Mutuality, respect for others, and the capacity to keep connecting and moving on are essential.
3. Curiosity is necessary for Transformation and for fundamentally different ways of operating.

4. The Overview Effect: Awareness that the whole of anything is greater than the sum of its parts.

When it comes to large, complex challenges (such as global warming, corruption, injustice, money being more important than people and sometimes life itself, multi-nation sovereignties preventing what's good for the whole world), there just don't seem to be procedural or structural changes that work to make things generally better. The CEQ is a way of shining a light, a golden lantern, on this planet-threatening situation as a tool for breakthrough collaboration.

Everyone in any situation has some level of Overview Awareness available. Though the comparison is difficult, imagine Low Overview frequencies to be more physical and known, while High Overview frequencies are aware of the whole, interrelated system, even its unknowns. This is the experience of seeing Earth from space as an example but can apply to any interrelated energy system.

The Collaborative Energy Quotient provides answers based on examples of typical everyday choices, challenges, or conflicts, such as:

- WHAT IS YOUR ENERGY LEVEL IN CHALLENGING COLLABORATIVE SITUATIONS? High, Medium, or Low?

- WHAT IS YOUR MUTUALITY LEVEL IN CHALLENGING COLLABORATIVE SITUATIONS? High, Medium, or Low?

- WHAT IS YOUR CURIOSITY LEVEL IN CHALLENGING COLLABORATIVE SITUATIONS? High, Medium, or Low?

THE COLLABORATIVE ENERGY QUOTIENT MISSION IS TO DEVELOP PERSONAL, EFFECTIVE WAYS TO CREATE AND SUSTAIN TRANSFORMATIONAL SHIFTS IN COLLABORATION AND ENABLE A POSITIVE FUTURE.

REQUEST THE FREE TEST ONLINE at SmithClinic.org

PRACTICAL APPLICATIONS

Article 1: The Camp David Retreat, Library of Professional Coaching. March 5, 2015, Mediative Coaching, Charles E. Smith

Abstract: The 1978 Camp David Retreat is an example of Real Thinking in the successful integration of present consciousness, coaching, mediation, and careful management of physical circumstances. From the severity of the challenges, the success of the event, and the sadness of later failures at the resolution, principles of Real Thinking were revealed.

The stakes were high; repeated wars between Israel and Arab states, acts of terrorism, denials of Israel's right to exist, and Arab civil liberties were persistent problems not resolved through "business as usual" diplomacy and avoidance. Parties continued to go their own way, settle for shallow relationships, and blur complexities with rhetoric.

Physical isolation and commitment to mediation were the keys. Repeated shifts in internal operations kept things moving, as well as a variety of approaches within and outside the traditional frameworks of advice, management, and diplomacy. U.S. President Jimmy Carter was the mediator.

Menachem Begin and Anwar Sadat, the leaders of Israel and Egypt, were the protagonists.

Guiding Principles:

1. Shared reality, uncharacteristic strategy, and periodic restructure.
2. Trusted and neutral mediator to orchestrate direct and indirect communication.
3. Normal hierarchical protocols between hierarchical levels and between functions are suspended.
4. Mediator controls time limits to introduce a sense of urgency.
5. Physical Isolation.
6. Information and Communication to The Outside World Are Suspended.
7. Interest-Based, Mediator Controlled Proposals Written Over and Over.
8. Spirituality of Key Actors Is a Required Foreground.
9. Planned Informality to Increase Accessibility and Spontaneous Behavior and Softening of Interpersonal Boundaries.
10. Continuous Juxtaposition of Peace with Its Opposite.
11. Many Meetings Among And Between Levels Of Authority At The Same Time.
12. Tension Release Mechanisms Are Easily Available.

Article 2: Mastering What Transforms: Dream the Impossible Dream and Go for It
—Eruditio, December 19, 2018, Charles E Smith

"Most civilization is based on cowardice. It's so easy to civilize by teaching cowardice. You water down the standards that could lead to bravery. You restrain the will. You regulate the

appetites. You fence in the horizons. You make a law for every movement. You deny the existence of chaos. You teach even the children to breathe slowly. You tame."
– Frank Herbert

Abstract: For a long time, we have been operating in ways that are used up and do not adequately address contemporary issues and concerns. People everywhere know it. This bankruptcy calls for a new code—a new Magna Carta, denying the rights given by the old social and economic order and declaring a new platform for the rights of men and women. Taken from fifty years of observation and experience in both successful and unsuccessful efforts to help individuals and organizations reach seemingly impossible goals, the article presents counter-intuitive roadmaps for leaders, teachers, and students, grounded in what is real for them. This 'kaleidoscope' of choices from points of view other than one's own often helps individuals and systems move from cultures of bureaucratic complexity to cultures of human mutuality and extraordinary performance.

1. The Problem: At this extraordinary time, the most important question we can ask is how to deal with massive disruption. The challenge is in how to change the nature, appearance, character, or function across business, education, community, leadership, governance, and relationships. The intent is to foster cultures of mutuality and bravery while succeeding in this new world, delivering on essential expectations, and achieving performance excellence.

2. The Tao of What Transforms
   "The words of truth are always paradoxical."
   Lao Tzu

'Mastering the Tao of What Transforms' is a form of evolutionary activism; a place from which to teach, train, mentor, and support leaders, scientists, teachers, advisors, mediators, and coaches who want to create collaborative, innovative systems for what is possible.

3. The Next Question: With respect to your own interests and concerns, what alternative models exist or can be conceived of to more effectively pursue the ideals of freedom, competence, security, prosperity, social equality, and mutuality? (The premise is that the universe consists of an infinite number of possibilities that do not exist until you ask a question).

4. An Alliance of Kindred Spirits: A movement based on leaders' existing or aspirational, spiritual, human, and pragmatic values and interests. Practically, this looks like the expansion of Present Awareness-based, Conscious Conversation in everyday life and work.

Article 3: Breaking Free: Bringing the Overview Effect to Life and Work

Eruditio, November 14, 2015,
by Charles Smith

Abstract: Upon breaking free of Earth's gravity and going to space, some astronauts experienced a surprising change in their perspective of life on Earth. Author Frank White named this phenomenon "The Overview Effect." Astronauts who experienced this were witnesses to a message about how to be with the planet and with each other. Their message about being "in the same boat" together points to an opportunity for many of us to break free of "the way it is" and create moments of transcendence that go beyond identity, individually and collectively. It is about shifting our point of view to see that what needs attention in our companies, communities, and relationships is always greater than the sum of the parts.

Article 4: Conversations that Matter

Eruditio, July 21, 2016,
by Charles Smith

Abstract: The article is about building a bridge between abstract discussions and conversations that matter. It is about transcending silos through everyday dialogue. It is about helping companies, governments, and communities operate in harmony with the way people really are, rather than the way authorities want them to be. It proposes that conversations that matter are a framework for turning cognitive dissonance into action. The object is to bring physical and relational coherence to life and work and to offer access to integrating high performance and human mutuality.

The premise is that a major problem with making a difference in the most challenging situations is abstraction itself, and that analysis, even when comprehensive, is necessarily linear and cannot produce a quantum shift in behavior, vision, strategy, and action. The case is made that conversations that matter can never find their way onto a PowerPoint. Conversations that matter call for the truth about people's actual experiences, with kindness and direct speaking at the same time. Timidity, fear, anger, power, and position inhibit conversations that matter. From global warming to corporate, governmental, and personal dysfunction, the cost of the unsaid truth is immense and ultimately deadly.

"At 40 years of age, I considered myself successful in my work in a global consumer goods company and in my family life with a wonderful wife and three children. I put this down to hard work and never gave up on anything I took on. When I met and worked with Charlie, I saw that I had only scratched the surface of what was possible for me and others. I saw that my success was both based on and massively limited by the 'winning formula' I had constructed and perfected over the years.

Seeing the world around me from the 'Avalon' (relationship) perspective alongside the 'Glastonbury' (structural) side opened up a journey of discovery and accomplishment that continues to this day, 40 years on. I still hold success important in what I do. However, I am conscious of the imposter it can be, and now pay far more attention to the quality and nature of my engagement and the energy this creates for myself and those around me.

I find this new book Charlie has given us to be a real treasure trove. Those committed to their own transformation will find the portal here."

Tony Turnbull, Executive Coach,
Former Procter and Gamble Manager

"Each page of <u>Transformational Practices</u> is a resonance to listen to that awakens humankind's original vision. Getting to where we want to go is not escaping where we find ourselves but resonating with the kind of Mach 25 escape velocity that frees us from the gravitational resignation of 'the way it is.' Each page is a postcard of a voyage taken through the ancient Huna science of Hawaii to a new perspective of Einstein's $E = MC^2$.

Transformational Practices is grounded in Merlin the Magician's seeing from the future when organizations and governments can lead far beyond only things that produce money and rhetoric. It's not about wishful thinking but about learning the perspective of the 'Overview Effect' of astronauts when they saw Earth with clarity as a place where we are in this together.

Transformational Practices is a good read and roadmap to 'Just do it.'"

Alexander Berlonghi, Founder of
Communications Dynamics International;
Special Event Risk Management; and
the Institute for the Practice of Ontology

POSTSCRIPT

A graduate of the Boston Public Latin School, Charlie holds a Bachelor's in Social Relations from Harvard College, an MBS from the Harvard Business School, a Ph.D. in Organizational Behavior from Case Western Reserve University, and a Certificate in Gestalt Methods from the Gestalt Institute of Cleveland.

He was a Visiting Associate Professor of Organizational Behavior at *Sir George Williams University* in Montreal and taught at the McGill Centre for Management Education.

A former President of the Harvard-Radcliff Club of New Mexico, Charlie was Executive Editor of *Transformational Magazine,* A Quarterly Road Map, and has published many articles at *The Library of Professional Coaching*, the *Library of Professional Psychology*, and *Eruditio,* a Journal of the World Academy of Art and Science.

Dr. Smith has published three additional books: *The Merlin Factor: Keys to the Corporate Kingdom, Navigating From the Future,* and *Don't be a Noodle in Someone Else's Soup.*

Made in United States
North Haven, CT
03 August 2022

22212829R10072